Greenhill Books

COMMANDO SUBALTERN AT WAR

In honour of
CAPTAIN RALPH PARKINSON-CUMINE MC, RM.
Killed in Korea
A fine officer and gentleman

COMMANDO SUBALTERN AT WAR

Royal Marine Operations in Yugoslavia and Italy, 1944–1945

W. G. JENKINS

GREENHILL BOOKS, LONDON
STACKPOLE BOOKS, PENNSYLVANIA

Greenhill Books

Commando Subaltern at War
First published 1996 by Greenhill Books, Lionel Leventhal Limited,
Park House, 1 Russell Gardens, London NW11 9NN
and
Stackpole Books, 5067 Ritter Road, Mechanicsburg, PA 17055, USA

British Library Cataloguing in Publication Data
Jenkins, W. G.
Commando subaltern at war: Royal Marine operations in
Yugoslavia and Italy, 1944–1945
1. World War, 1939–1945 – Commando operations – Italy
2. World War, 1939–1945 – Commando operations – Yugoslavia
3. World War, 1939–1945 – Personal narratives, British
I. Title
940.5′412′41

ISBN 1–85367–231–9

Library of Congress Cataloging-in-Publication Data
Jenkins, W. G. (William G.)
Commando subaltern at war: Royal Marine operations in Yugoslavia
and Italy, 1944–1945 / by W. G. Jenkins.
184p. 24cm.
ISBN 1–85367–231–9
1. Jenkins, W. G. (William G.) 2. World War, 1939–1945 –
– Campaigns – Yugoslavia. 3. World War, 1939–1945 – Campaigns – Italy.
4. World War, 1939–1945 – Personal narratives, British. 5. Great Britain. Royal
Marines. Royal Marine Commando, 43rd – History. 6. Great Britain. Royal
Marines – Biography. 7. Marines – Great Britain – Biography. I. Title.
D766.6.J395 1996
940.54′8141 – dc20
95–47814
CIP

Typeset by Nene Phototypesetters, Northampton
Printed and bound in Great Britain
by Bookcraft (Bath) Limited, Midsomer Norton

Contents

List of Illustrations

List of Maps and Diagrams

Foreword

A fascinating account of the author's experience of wartime training and operations and of his use of this experience in peacetime military training and adventure training after the war as a civilian lecturer at Sandhurst. His natural modesty hides the fact that, for his action in northern Italy in 1945, he was awarded the DSO – an unusual award for a subaltern and one of the two youngest such awards to a Royal Marine officer in the Second World War.

It is all of interest; perhaps the most unusual chapters cover Bill Jenkins's time on the Dalmatian islands and in Yugoslavia, though his graphic account of operations in Italy at the end of the war is second to none.

But read it all – it is well worth while.

I am reminded of the memorial plaque in the old British naval cemetery on Vis, the last lines of which read:

> 'Life to be sure is nothing much to lose
> But young men think it is and we were young'

Major General R.B. Loudoun CB OBE
1996

Acknowledgements

My thanks to John Keegan, who, after reading a fuller autobiography, advised me to concentrate on the military theme. Lionel Leventhal's constructive comments enabled me to modify the structure. Desmond Clark, who was mainly responsible for producing *Nothing Much to Lose* (privately printed; see bibliography), passed on much practical advice. Cecily Parkinson-Cumine provided my detailed description of the Argenta action.

For authoritative accounts of the war-time political situation in Yugoslavia I referred to *Eastern Approaches* by Sir Fitzroy Maclean and *The Embattled Mountain* by F.W.D. Deakin.

The Trustees of the Imperial War Museum, London, have given permission for the reproduction of twenty-five photographs from their Archives. Other photographs have been contributed by Michael McConville, and I am indebted to John and Jeff Gordon for providing me with five prints from the record of the activities of Second Battalion RM and 43 RM Commando which they have collected and mounted in honour of their father, who served in both units. Michael Nicklinson prepared the map-work for publication, and my daughter Lesley came up with the caption for the identity discs.

Stan Buckmaster and Charles Messenger have given permission for the account of the first Solta operation, published originally in *The Commandos 1940 to 1946*, to be included. Some of the material in this book has been published in the *British Army Review* – 'Commando Operations in Yugoslavia' in April 1987 and 'Training in Leadership on the Rowallan Course' in August 1982. A full account of the Everest expedition appeared in the December 1984 issue. The Appendix on the Brathay Exploration Group has been written by Brian Ware OBE, who led the first field-work expedition in 1947. He has directed and guided the Group right up to the present time.

As a lowly subaltern I hardly expected to receive help from two Generals. Major General Bob Loudoun, who has contributed the Foreword, served in 43 RM Commando right from the start – it was formed in August 1943 – and took part in every operation from Anzio to Argenta. Lieutenant General Sir Robert Ross KCB OBE, the present Commandant General Royal Marines, has kindly offered to write a review of the book for the *The Globe and Laurel*.

Most of all I must thank Mrs Jacqueline Cundell for her help and encouragement. She dealt patiently and efficiently on her word processor with innumerable revisions, and her optimism as to a successful outcome never faltered.

Introduction

Fifty years on, memories of events during the spells of action still remain clear. Notes jotted down in a couple of Field Message books have provided reminders of less exciting times, and other contemporary written material authenticates details which have been included. Official histories and other post-war books have given me a better understanding of the higher strategic situation in Italy and the Balkans. At the time we had no idea at unit level as to what was going on behind the scenes.

Although my period of active service was comparatively short – some nine months in all – I gained experience of three very different types of military situation. When 43 RM Commando first landed on the Yugoslav island of Vis in February 1944, well-equipped German forces had been steadily reoccupying the other Dalmatian islands after the Italian surrender in September 1943. Tito's Partisan forces defending the island welcomed British support, and the expected German assault did not take place. Friendly relations were established between us, which led to offensive operations against the German garrisons on the other islands. These were just what we had been trained for – amphibious landings; quick approach marches; attacks utilising mainly our own resources; and withdrawal within a limited time to minimise on logistical support.

In October 1944 the Commando landed at Dubrovnik to provide protection for artillery units. The military situation had changed dramatically, as the Germans were retreating from Greece and Albania. Many vulnerable targets were presented as their columns followed the restricted routes through Montenegro, but practically all our proposals for offensive operations were blocked by the Partisans. They wanted artillery and air support, but had no wish for British assault troops to take any credit at that stage. We were moved around from bivouac to bivouac on the barren upland plateau in bitter climatic conditions without the satisfaction of getting to grips with the enemy. There are often frustrating times on active service. With liberation of Yugoslavia within sight, Tito was determined to establish control over the whole country with a Communist regime after the war. His two main bargaining points were that through their resistance his Partisans had held down considerable German forces from being used elsewhere, and that they had won their own freedom.

In Yugoslavia we were part of an independent, light, mobile force, so it was a complete contrast to be posted into the front line when we returned to Italy. The entrenched positions had been static for some time, and our sector was on the extreme east, south of Lake Comacchio. On 2 April 1945 2 Commando

15

Brigade launched the first preliminary attack in the Eighth Army's spring offensive which, with the American Fifth Army pushing forward on the west, brought about the surrender of Germany's Army Group C on 2 May 1945.

I had the advantage of youth in dealing with war, which I treated as an exciting game. The dark side was that things that would normally be unacceptable – arbitrary death, mutilation, destruction and suffering – became commonplace. My temperament was such that they left no mental scars, but war is senseless. Nevertheless military training and action equip one to deal with difficult situations. I put this experience to constructive use after the war by taking parties of young men to remote areas to carry out useful scientific field-work. The challenges which occur away from the trappings of so-called civilisation are set by nature, not by shells, mines and bullets. Surmounting the difficulties achieved the same close camaraderie of wartime without the cost in lives and wounds.

Prologue

One evening in early August 1944 nine Royal Marine officers, of whom I was one, embarked on a 'Jug' schooner in Molfetta harbour, on Italy's Adriatic coast, where we joined a group of Partisans. Thoughts about a possible encounter with a German 'E' boat were soon forgotten, as our companions had brought plenty of drink on board, and we had a convivial trip across the Adriatic. A semi-profile framed photograph of a good-looking young man caught my attention. The wide brow, steady eyes, long straight nose, and firm chin reminded me of the late actor Leslie Howard. The Partisans told me that his name was Ivo Ribar, and they spoke passionately about him in Serbo-Croat, but all that I could gather from their gestures was that he had been killed. Shortly after dawn we chugged past two small forts perched on headlands on either side of the entrance to the picturesque little harbour of Vis. It was a unique introduction to a fascinating period of active service.

Almost a year earlier, on 17 September 1943, Brigadier Fitzroy Maclean had parachuted into Bosnia as the personal representative of the Prime Minister to make contact with Tito at his HQ at Jajce. After making a thorough first-hand assessment of the Partisan situation he decided that in order to obtain material support it was necessary for him to go back to report personally. Tito asked if two Partisan delegates, Ivo Ribar and Miloje Milojevic, could accompany him. Although he realised that this would cause diplomatic problems, as Britain had given official recognition to the Royal Yugoslav government-in-exile, Maclean signalled back this request. After some delay the reply ordered him to return to Cairo immediately, but said that the Partisan delegates could follow later if required.

The Germans were re-establishing control along the Adriatic coast after the Italian surrender, but Maclean got through on foot from Jajce to the small settlement of Baska Voda, not far from Split. Fishing boats ferried him first to Hvar, and then to Vis. There he sent a signal for the Navy to pick him up, and a motor launch took him across to Bari. He was whisked on to an aeroplane, and flown to Cairo. The Foreign Secretary, Anthony Eden, was there on his way back from Moscow. Maclean was able to give him both a verbal and a written report.

His next task was to get the Partisan delegates out to Cairo, as Churchill himself would be there shortly. After flying back to Italy, Maclean managed to persuade the RAF to provide him with a Baltimore light bomber, as the Partisans had constructed a rough airstrip near Glamoc. The Americans agreed to protect it with an escort of Lightning fighters. There was sunshine across the Adriatic, but when they crossed over the Dinaric Alps they became engulfed in a blinding snowstorm – it was late November – and it was impossible to land. The next day exactly the same thing happened. On the third attempt the bomber went over unescorted, and although the pilot took considerable risks in trying to get down through the murk, he had to turn back yet again. Captain Bill Deakin, who had been parachuted in earlier to make contact with the Partisans, then signalled from Bosnia that a Croat crew had deserted to the Partisans with a small Dornier, and that they would fly out in that. The plane was on the Glamoc airstrip with its engines running when a German Henschel suddenly appeared low over the crest of the hill. A bomb scored a direct hit on the Dornier, and the pilot machine-gunned the field. Ivo Ribar was killed instantly, as were two members of the British Mission.

Ivo Lola Ribar became an ardent Communist when he was a student at Belgrade University. Djilas chose him to head the Youth Organisation just before the war, and Tito included him in his underground Central Committee. His intelligence and courage in operations against the Axis Forces made him a leading figure among the Partisans. After his death he became a hero of the National Liberation Movement, symbolising the contribution of youth. That is what the Partisans on the schooner had been trying to tell me.

When the weather cleared, Maclean got hold of a troop-carrying Dakota and half a squadron of escort Lightnings and set off yet again. The plane was piloted on the outward flight by Wing Commander John Selby DSO DFC who was going out to join Maclean's Mission. This time they were able to pick up the signal flares on the Glamoc airstrip, and the first landing on enemy-occupied Yugoslav territory was made in broad daylight. A wounded Miloje Milojevic was loaded on board on a stretcher, and Vlatco Velebit replaced Lola. They flew to Bari, and then on to Alexandria in the same Dakota. The Prime Minister had arrived from Teheran, so Maclean was able to meet him. Churchill had read Maclean's report, which had influenced his discussions with Roosevelt and Stalin. Now he questioned Fitzroy closely as to the relative merits of the Royalist Cetniks and the Partisans. What he heard confirmed his decision to give full support to the latter, despite their strong orientation towards the Soviet Union.

By the time that we arrived, the small island of Vis had been developed into a flourishing base for combined operations, where Allied naval, ground and air force units lived in close proximity to our Partisan allies. My preparation for an active role had been long and thorough, and it stood me in very good stead.

* * *

It had started in boyhood, when I was a keen Boy Scout. I first donned military uniform in 1939, as a member of the Blundells School Officer Training

Corps. The school tailor still fitted us out with the First World War type of uniform – tunic with round brass buttons down the front and hooks and eyes for the close-fitting collar; broad breeches with puttees to the knee; and round peaked cap with the brown cap-badge of the Devonshire Regiment. We had Lee-Enfield rifles with the long bayonet, and the old-pattern broader webbing. Eventually we were issued with the new battledress and fore-and-aft forage caps. Whatever reservations we had about abandoning tradition soon went when there were no buttons to clean, and the web gaiters buckled on much more quickly than winding on puttees.

Public school was a useful apprenticeship for the armed forces. The system of punishments taught us as Juniors to obey the rules and to respect authority. As Seniors we were given opportunities to exercise responsibility and to show leadership. Games encouraged a strong will to win, but to win fairly through teamwork, and the OTC gave an early introduction to drill, fieldcraft, map-reading and shooting. After passing Certificate 'A' I became a cadet NCO, and trained the Juniors.

In 1939 I was too young to bother much with international affairs, but my father looked more and more serious when we listened to the news. Then came the invasion of Poland and two days later Chamberlain's monotone announce-ment that we were at war, followed by the wail of air-raid sirens, which was disconcerting right at the start. It proved to be a false alarm as very little happened during the months of the 'Phoney War', and the strange limbo atmosphere was reflected in such shallow patriotic songs as 'We're gonna hang out the washing on the Siegfried Line' and 'Run, rabbit, run'. We got used to the blackout, and signposts disappeared from the roads.

The spell was broken when the Germans outflanked the Maginot Line at Sedan. I distinctly recall following the progress of events in the newspaper maps. A small black bulge became successively larger and larger until broad black arrows broke out towards the coast. Then came the anxious days of the Dunkirk evacuation, and the subsequent rapid fall of France.

We were now on our own but morale was strong, stirred by the growling defiance and memorable phrases of Churchill's broadcasts, and his unshakable conviction that his countrymen had the fortitude to stand up to forthcoming assaults. Food rationing, sweet rationing, clothing coupons and petrol coupons dominated our day-to-day lives. When I played rugby at the Royal Naval College, Dartmouth, it is not the game that I remember but the individual pats of butter and helpings of jam which we had for tea afterwards. The cadets were on naval rations, and for us this was almost as much as for a week. At night there was the slightly irregular rumble of Dornier bombers passing overhead on their way to Bristol, Swansea or Liverpool. Once the engine noise was much louder, indicating that an aircraft was flying low. Surprisingly there were two tremendous explosions. The pilot must have ditched his bombs after getting into difficulties. Early next morning I was on my bike hunting for the craters, which turned out to be quite close, so I proudly brought back some useless pieces of shrapnel and a nose-cone. During the 'Baedeker' raids we saw the glow in the sky when Exeter got its pounding fifteen miles to the south. I had to go there two days later, and it was sad to see the damage to the cathedral. What struck me most were the smouldering remains of a grain store: the warm, sickly smell hanging heavy in the air emitted an aura of destruction and death,

It was my good fortune that there was an excellent Geography master at Blundells, Wansborough French. In the sixth form he proved most innovative and helpful. The Macbride Open Scholarship only comes up every three years, and despite the fact that it was a year early for me, WWF let me have a go. At the age of sixteen and three-quarters I sat the exam papers at Oxford in January 1942. There was not much competition in the middle of the war and to everyone's complete surprise I was given the award. It was pleasing to save my father some expense, as schoolmasters were not paid much at that time.

I went up to Hertford College, Oxford, at the beginning of October 1942. Less time was available for study as we had to do two and a half days military training each week – many people were up on six-month Services courses. For some time I had been attracted to the Navy, and the University Naval Division was being formed for the first time, so I was an original entrant. The bell-bottom rig hugs the figure closely, and I wondered how fat sailors managed. When we had to plough through the welter of material in the 'Manual of Seamanship' I became a little less enamoured.

At my medical I was not sure whether my eyesight was good enough for the Navy, but I passed, so I was cock-a-hoop. The last check was for colour vision, and to my great surprise I was informed that I was slightly colour-blind. I was unable to decipher the correct figures among the jumble of small coloured circles. At that time the regulations for the Royal Marines were not quite so strict, so I accepted the offer to join, though I knew little about them.

Because of my OTC experience I was in the 'Y' scheme, which earmarked candidates for officer training, but I decided to transfer to the University Senior Training Corps for my last two terms, as I could get Certificate 'B', a more advanced qualification in infantry command, which would be useful now that I had enlisted in the Marines.

The memorable personality was CSM Jim Cowley of the Coldstream Guards, who had joined the Parachute Regiment. On a flying course he had crashed in a light aircraft, so his posting to Oxford was to give him time to recover fully from his injuries. He had the right touch in handling undergraduates, combining discipline with a sense of humour, so we produced good drill, and we profited from all aspects of the training. One incident is etched clearly in my mind. In fieldcraft we were practising monkey-crawl on all-fours, and I decided to be really keen, so when he called a halt I was about twenty yards in front of the rest, feeling pleased with myself. With a twinkle in his eye he turned us about, and said that the last man back to the start-line would have to do it again. I went all-out and caught up and passed the rear men. It was a subtle way of bringing home that life is not always fair, and that injustice can induce a positive response. Prophetically he gave me the nickname 'Commando'. After the war I heard that he had won the Distinguished Conduct Medal when he returned to active service in Europe.

Every fortnight we went on a ten-mile speed march out along the Cowley Road to the Oxford bypass which we followed round to come back down the Banbury Road. This involved doubling and marching alternately, which tested our stamina, as we wore webbing and carried rifles. We generally got round in about an hour and forty minutes. The course finished with a twelve-day camp at Churn on Blewbury Down after the end of the summer term, and this culminated in two platoon attacks using live ammunition. I was appointed to command the second one, and by that time I had plenty of confidence, so my orders were clear, and everything was going well. The fire section and the 2-inch mortar gave covering fire on the objective as the assault sections ran in on their final advance. The mortar was firing high trajectory, and suddenly there was the sharp crack of an explosion only yards from those of us in the centre of the extended line – a faulty bomb had fallen short. The only person to be hit by shrapnel was the OC of the university contingent, Major Keith, who was following just behind. I immediately called off the attack and went to his assistance. He had a nasty leg wound which I bound up with my field dressing before arranging by wireless for a vehicle to take him to hospital. I remember how calmly he accepted the unfortunate accident, but it was a most unkind cut after all that he had done to help us, and took the edge off our return to Oxford. Next day we dispersed to our respective homes, but it was not long before the Marines got hold of me.

CHAPTER 1

From Other Rank to Officer

On 9 August 1943 I reported at Lympstone Barracks near Exmouth, swore my oath of allegiance to the King, and became PO/X 117717 Marine Jenkins W.G. When I was standing naked for the initial medical inspection an orderly pulled my foreskin back to check on personal hygiene down to the last detail – routine for him, but an unexpected shock for me. We were inoculated against TAB, TT and smallpox, but I was slow to realise that this may have accounted for my initial feeling of lethargy. At Churn Camp there had been the cheerful companionship of undergraduate friends, and we had a relaxed relationship with our NCO instructors and the officers. Now one had to hold one's own in a barrack room with twenty or more strangers who had different backgrounds, regional accents and customs. At the camp I had been in charge of thirty-eight cadets but now I was just a name and number under the firm control of NCOs and trained long-service Marines, who made us conform to the strict standards demanded by the depot. Officers were remote figures who carried out inspections. It was a regression to the first year at school, as we had to start again at the bottom of the pile.

We were kept busy all day, with a great deal of drill, plus weapon training and PT. Donald Murray (another Oxford man) and I had to adapt quickly from guardsman stamping to bringing the heel in slickly for Marine drill. Evenings were spent ironing uniform (a touch of soap on the insides of battle-dress creases) and cleaning equipment and weapons. There were plenty of fatigues and duties. Once when washing up after dinner I came across a large tin tray still almost full of rice pudding, so I piled in quickly. Not for long. There was a thick layer of herring underneath which had not been cleaned off after breakfast! I was paid the princely sum of twenty shillings a week, but I managed easily on this, partly because I had always had to be careful with money, partly because I did not smoke or drink much, and partly because we had no free time. When we had completed the weeks of basic training (far less than the regular King's Squads had to do) we were deemed fit to appear in public in Royal Marine uniform. Only then did the almost-forgotten Y scheme come into effect, and Donald and I were posted to a pre-OCTU (Officer Cadet Training Unit) course at Deal.

Here there was even more pressure, both mental and physical, and at times we were deliberately messed about, as the aim was to weed people out. We young men realised what was going on and put up with it, but the NCOs who were going for a commission found it more difficult to accept such treatment, and quite a few of them applied for RTU (Return to Unit). Donald Murray came very close to doing so. On a long exercise, a testing experience which suited their purposes well was to send us in batches through a large drain about thirty yards long which was half full of sludge. The confined space necessitated bending forward, making it awkward to carry one's weapon (I had a Bren light machine gun), and impossible to avoid getting absolutely filthy. The instructors were stationed at either end and let off thunderflashes, which made one hell of a bang. I was not bothered, but this noise, coupled with feelings of claustrophobia, had a serious effect on two or three people, who emerged in a really distressed condition, from which they did not recover for some hours. We got back to barracks late, to be informed that there would be a full kit inspection at nine o'clock the next morning. Everything had to be scrubbed, as the fine silt had got everywhere, and we were up all night drying things off. Next morning, as the platoon commander moved across to hand the large cardboard layout check to Donald, he trod on his groundsheet. After checking that all the items were in order he pointed to some dirt left by the footprint and ordered another inspection for six o'clock. Donald flung down the chart towards him, but fortunately did not do anything more drastic. Two of us had to latch on to him all day to prevent him from pulling out, as he was completely 'chokker' (Marine slang for 'fed up'). We laid out his kit for him, and after much persuasion managed to get him to turn up, but it was touch and go. The platoon commander was not a popular man, but he was only doing his duty. As a matter of fact this course was probably the most useful part of our officer training, as it made us fully aware of the consequences of bad man-management, and the deeply implanted memories guided us when it came to handling our own men later on.

My right arm started to swell up like a balloon but I did not report sick as I was concerned that I might be put back to go through the mill again. On parade one morning I had a buzzing in my ears, and the next thing I knew I was on the ground, and someone was loosening my collar. My friends told me that I went down like a log, standing stiffly to attention. I was carted off to the sick bay where the blood poisoning was cleared up in about a week, and I was allowed to rejoin the course.

Deal provided the ultimate in military bullshit. For barrack room inspections there was a unique blanket layout. They had to be folded lengthways, and then wrapped round in a Swiss roll so that sixteen neat narrow folds faced the front, with all ends carefully butted so as not to show. There were two large brass scuttles full of coal, which of course was never used. We expected to clean the scuttles, but whitewashing the tops of the pieces of coal came as a bit of a surprise! Big German guns were engaged in sporadic cross-Channel shelling and when this happened at night the alarm went and the orders were to go down to the shelters. I took a chance and stayed comfortably in bed – no shells or NCOs descended on me.

The next posting was to OCTU at Thurlestone, where the Marines had taken over a hotel set on a clifftop on the south Devon coast. This course was intensive but constructive, with the emphasis on leadership, orders, platoon exercises, PT, patrolling and map-reading. On HO 23 we were being trained for Hostilities Only, and we would receive temporary commissions. There was a small Regular batch who were doing one phase of an eighteen-month course which included gunnery prior to serving on 'big ships'. They used the Officers' Mess and were encouraged to pursue up-stage activities such as horseriding, so we saw little of them. There was precious little cooperative spirit on HO 23 as so many of the cadets were mainly concerned as to how well they were doing individually, and whether they would pass, and towards the end this edgy atmosphere started to get to me as well.

Prior to one night patrol exercise, Dick Thornton and I obtained a pass to visit the Links Hotel on the golf course, and I poured a double rum into a small bottle before we left. My room-mates had left one-sixth of the floor for me to scrub, but I managed to do this as well as get ready. Leading my patrol across Dartmoor in the darkness of the early hours, I was in a dilemma, as there was not enough rum to pass back for the whole section, so I decided to swig it myself. There was some muttering as following noses picked up the smell.

Tactics were taken to battalion level, and we were taught the essentials of military law, both of which involved indoor lectures. After all the physical activity I frequently fell asleep. The major in charge of the course used to throw chalk at me, but he invariably missed and hit someone else. Lieutenant Colonel Martin Price had a more effective technique. Half-way through a lecture he suddenly picked up the blackboard and hurled it across the dais. All of us instantly became wide awake. He had won a DSO at Madagascar in May 1942 when as a captain he landed with his ship's detachment from the battle-ship *Ramillies* and secured Antsirane opposite Diego Suarez (another capture of a strategic harbour from Vichy France).

I see from the group photograph that seventy-five of us got through. Most people were posted to landing-craft duties, as preparations for D-Day were building up. Six of us were selected for Commando training. We had no say in this, but with the die cast I felt a thrill that I would be training for the élite branch of the Corps.

CHAPTER 2

Gaining the Green Beret at Achnacarry

Now that there was a pip on the shoulder, the top of the battledress was pressed back to be worn with a collar and tie instead of being clipped at the neck. A grant (£55) enabled us to be kitted out by John Jones tailors with KSD (Khaki Service Dress), Sam Browne cross-over belt, officer's greatcoat, brown shoes, round service cap, leather gloves, and leather swagger cane. Not for us, though, the comfort of an old-established officers' mess. We were posted to Dalditch, a Nissen hut camp on top of Woodbury Common just east of the Exe estuary. It was a cold February in 1944, and the winds whistled piercingly through, especially into the ablutions and latrines, which were only semi-enclosed. With the freezing weather there was often no hot water.

Assault courses, death-slides, river crossings, speed-marches, unarmed combat, and group PT with tree-trunks were the order of the day, so we spent most of our time in denims, and KSD was seldom worn. We gave little thought to it, but it must have been dangerous rigging the death-slides, as we climbed the highest pines to tie on the heavy ropes. Easing out to launch oneself with a toggle rope was the tricky bit, but the descents were enjoyable. Toggle ropes were also used to construct V-span bridges. With the weight of full fighting order and a weapon slung round the neck, one had to push apart the upper ropes in order to slide the feet forward, and the longer the distance the more awkwardly the contraption swung. Weekends were more relaxed than at Thurlestone, so we raised a rugby team to play local fixtures. An enthusiastic member was Maurice Wood, the naval chaplain, who went on to become Bishop of Norwich. One rather sad figure was a short dumpy major who had acquitted himself very well as a young subaltern in the Zeebrugge raid in 1918. During the inter-war period he had remained a bachelor, promotion had passed him by, boredom had been offset by drink, and he had ended up in this backwater administering a succession of eager youngsters going through.

A very useful part of the training was that each young officer was allowed to run his own exercise. My project was to capture Dawlish railway station. I had to take responsibility for everything – liaison with the station master to get his permission, and to avoid the trains; the booking of an assault landing craft; timings for tides and length of voyage, and details on meals, dress and equipment. I was given a platoon of Marines, and we began down on the Exe shoreline by practising embarkation and disembarkation drills, taking up all-round defence, and carrying out strategic withdrawal. To my relief the day of the exercise dawned fine, with the sea not too rough. We marched tactically to the RV (rendezvous point) with the landing craft and slapped our way through the waves for some time until identifiable landmarks eventually came in sight. The landing craft surged in to the beach, the ramp went down, and we stormed up a slipway, to the amazement of the people who were about. As soon as I was able to get a good view of the ground I designated specific areas and arcs of fire to each section commander and platoon HQ, and they spread out to take up their positions. We did not disturb the peace by firing blanks. With the place secure I strode down the platform to thank the station master personally for his cooperation. Then I went round inspecting fire positions before firing off a Verey light as the signal for withdrawal. Each small group covered the other in turn back to the landing craft. The men had not previously taken part in a combined operation, so an assault from the sea was a new experience for them (and for me). As we chugged back I felt satisfied with a job well done, and when we returned to camp I made sure that they all had a hot meal.

I was sent on a week's special course at the London District School of Street Fighting in Battersea, where a large area had been evacuated after being severely bombed. It was a hair-raising affair. Everything was booby-trapped, and they waited to see how many charges we exploded before they showed us how they were set. We used live 'bee-hive' explosive charges to blast through internally down a line of council houses to clear each building in turn. The noise and the rubble and the dust made things very realistic. We worked in pairs and shouted to cover each other as we burst into rooms and got our backs to a wall to shoot at targets. Outside we had to keep as flat as possible when we scrambled over the tops of walls, or thunderflashes were the penalty. Thankfully I was never involved in house to house fighting, as it is a lethal business, but I realise what both sides had to endure at Cassino, Stalingrad and Berlin. There was one day of relief, when the theoretical alternatives were to learn how to drive a train, or how to blow up Battersea Power Station. Much to my chagrin there was no choice in our case – the senior NCOs got the train, as officers on previous courses had misbehaved by blowing the whistle too often. So we were taken into the power station to be shown the vital machinery where explosive charges would do maximum damage.

From Dalditch we were sent to another Nissen hut establishment, Gibraltar Camp at Llanegryn just north of Tywyn. Here we added rock climbing to our training activities, and I learned to drive a motor bike. One day we were taken to watch a RM Commando carrying out a full-scale live-firing attack in preparation for D-Day. While we were standing at our vantage point we suddenly realised that bullets were thudding into the hillside all around us. Miraculously no one was hit, but there must have been a serious error in target indication, as it was not intended for us to receive such a close baptism of fire.

On one trip I called in at the hotel at Tal-y-Llyn, which had few visitors in those days, and enjoyed the rare treat of fresh eggs, farmhouse butter and home-baked Welsh scones.

After this good preparation the moment of truth came for me in May 1944 – the chance to qualify for the coveted green beret at Achnacarry. As the only officer, I was in charge of the draft, and was warned that there were two men with criminal records who might go AWOL (absent without leave). In view of this, when the train was held up in Glasgow I got out and walked up and down the platform. My pistol was slung in a holster on my right hip, and one wag started to sing 'Pistol-packin' Momma, lay that pistol down'. It was good-humouredly taken up until the whole draft was belting out the song, which made me grin. When we mustered at Spean Bridge, sure enough the two men were missing. They must have climbed out of the other side of the train and crossed the lines, but I could hardly have put them under close supervision just on suspicion.

The introduction to the Commando Basic Training Centre was typical. We were formed up in squads with our baggage (myself with a suitcase instead of a kit bag) and were then harried along a fast speed-march down the eight miles to Achnacarry. This was the seat of Donald Cameron of Lochiel, and while we were there we wore a circle of his tartan behind our Globe and Laurel cap-badge. As we doubled along the final stretch towards the entrance to the camp our attention was caught by a line of graves with white crosses alongside the road. Later inspection revealed that they were training aids – 'This man died from sky-lining himself'. 'This man failed to detect mines at night'; a dramatic way to bring the lessons home. In point of fact, forty men did lose their lives in training over the four years that CBTC was in operation. Outside the gate we were halted, uniforms were straightened, bags tucked under the left arm, and we marched in with parade ground precision.

Everything at CBTC was that much tougher. The walls on the obstacle course were 8 ft instead of 6 ft; speed-marches were fifteen miles instead of ten; and Ben Nevis was higher than the mountains in Wales. One essential principle that none of us ever forgot was to help each other: to work in pairs as 'me and my pal'. This was particularly important on the 8 ft wall. The first man could get a good push-up from cupped hands, and he stayed on top. For the second it was more difficult. He took a run and lunged up with one foot on the wall for his partner to grab him and heave, so that he could get his arms over the top. Roles were reversed each time. A high proportion of the exercises involved live firing, and we became used to priming and throwing Mills bombs. The emphasis was on effective marksmanship – metal plates had to be knocked down before we were allowed forward. Always it was one man covering the other, and when it came to house clearance I was in my element. On a night infiltration exercise I spotted our instructor, a Parachute Regiment captain, and decided to stalk up and pounce on him. This was an unwise move. After his initial surprise he got the better of me in the tussle, and I ended up half-throttled with a vice-like arm-lock round my throat. He kept up the pressure long enough to show who was boss, and then allowed me to carry on. There was still a long way to go, and the encounter left me exhausted, but I persevered.

For abseiling we used the 35 ft-high walls of Achnacarry House. The start was awkward, edging out backwards over the balustrade to plant one's feet on the wall, and the secret was to lean back as much as possible. At that time we wrapped the rope over the shoulder and round the thigh, but in battledress this created too much friction for a fast descent. Nowadays a web harness can be buckled on, and by attaching a karabiner one can whistle down in big bounds. In the mountains one climb was a diagonal ascent up a rock-face which was not too difficult – provided one had a head for heights. The man in front of me obviously did not. He was pressing his body tightly to the rock, making it difficult to see handholds and footholds, so I had to talk him on to them, and he was reluctant to give up one hold for the next. Three-quarters of the way up was the crux, where a boss of rock had to be rounded. I explained the technique to him – he had to stand out a bit on his good right foothold, reach round for a handhold, and then it was essential to shift his weight forward as he moved his left foot to the ledge on the other side. The snag was that this revealed the view down, and when he finally screwed himself up to make the move he kept too close to the rock, failed to shift his weight, and got spread-eagled round the boss, albeit with good holds. I sensed the danger signs of his muscles beginning to tremble and was moving forward to try to lend a hand when to my amazement he gave a little gasp and just let go. The instructor was standing on top of the boss about eight feet above with a safety rope attached to a tree, but this was useless in the circumstances. By admitting he could not do it, he would have been hauled up. But he chose to overcome his fear and suffered for his courage. It was a long drop, and he got badly smashed up on the lower slopes, but we were relieved to hear later that he survived. The rest of us had to get off the face, and I had no difficulty with the move.

The pyrotechnics for the final exercise provided us with battle inoculation. In an assault across Loch Ailort the emphasis was on speed. Each group was timed, to set up the elements of team-work and competition. Weapons were stowed in the centre of assault boats, and eight of us took up our positions on each side. As we paddled across, Bren-guns fired tracer overhead so that we kept our heads low, and bullets hit the water on fixed lines to the flanks to make us steer straight. As we jumped out to carry the boats up the beach, the instructors threw thunderflashes and smoke grenades, and sappers let off noisy charges all the time we were ashore. Grabbing our weapons, we had to adopt good fire positions to knock down the white metal plates before the instructors shouted us forward, and this process was repeated several times prior to the final bayonet charge against straw-filled figures on the objective. When the instructors were satisfied that the position had been properly cleared, they gave the signal to withdraw and we rushed back to the boats, stowed weapons, launched, climbed into our positions, and paddled back under renewed fire from the Brens.

My pleasure when told that I had passed turned to trepidation when a message came that the redoubtable Charlie Vaughan wanted to see me. The Commandant was a big, bluff, hearty man who had been commissioned after rising to RSM in The Buffs. He was now a Lieutenant Colonel, and no man did more to inculcate the Commando spirit of doing things better and with more determination and initiative than down-to-earth Charlie, who really understood men, and knew how to get the best out of them. Apprehensively I knocked on his door, marched into the room, and saluted. He got up, shook my hand with a jovial smile, and to my great surprise said that I had done well, and that he was considering having me as an instructor. I received this news with mixed feelings. It was certainly an honour, but I wanted to get to a unit rather than remain in the training field. People who spent some time at Achnacarry tended to become a bit 'gung-ho'. The decision was not immediate, as he had decided to send me on a Cliff Assault Course.

The very next morning I travelled from the wilds of Scotland to the tip of Cornwall with one of the instructors, CSM 'Spider' Leach. The Commandos had a system of allowances for 'civvy billets' so, one day fledged, I found a hotel room in Carbis Bay. Spider's pretty little wife Marion was living with her parents in St Ives, so he was well away. Before he joined up he had been a steeplejack on the tin-mine chimneys, so for him the climbs were a doddle, but I had done little rock-face stuff. For the first part of each pitch I was able to follow his moves, but too often he then went out of sight and I had to work things out for myself. There was the knowledge that he would hold me on the rope if I fell off, but fortunately I did not do so. Commando Ridge, opposite the higher Bosigran face, was a good starting point to learn most of the skills. There was a tricky little vertical crack at sea level, where the rock was slippery; then some chimneying; and then an exposed horizontal traverse with minimum fingerholds. On the crests (less than a foot wide) of a couple of gendarmes we stood upright to gain confidence in balance and exposure, as there was nothing but space all around, and the jagged coastline far below. (Years later I took parties of cadets from Sandhurst down to these climbs as part of their Adventure Training. The last occasion was in 1985 – forty-one years on – and I stood upright on the gendarmes for old time's sake.)

Other climbing areas we used were at Sennen, Land's End, and Chair Ladder, where the southern cliffs rise steeply straight from the sea for the highest routes. We were issued with heavy climbing boots with metal tri-coonies fixed round the welts, and were taught to keep our heels out and high for the small teeth to bite best. I was touched that Spider took the trouble to scrounge a set of tri-coonies from the store to give to me. Nowadays light, narrow, close-fitting climbing boots with firm rubber soles give very good friction on dry rock, and make climbing much easier.

Less specialist were the cliff assaults that we practised at Kynance Cove on the Lizard. There were machines which fired up three-pronged grappling irons with a rope attached, and we jiggled them until we felt them bite, hoping that after a strong tug they were safely lodged before we ascended. In addition some good climbers went up with ropes paying out from wicker baskets on their backs, which they secured at the top. As soon as a rope had been fixed by one of these methods a section went up quickly by pulling hand over hand, as the footholds were generally quite good. Withdrawal was also fast, as the first wave abseiled down, and then anchored the ropes as death-slides for the rest to shoot down rapidly, using karabiners instead of toggle ropes. As a geographer I was interested in the serpentine crystalline rocks, but the rest were little concerned with the geomorphological changes that had fashioned the cliffs that they had to climb.

Landing from dories was the third activity, and we took it in turn to act as bowman. The coxswain eased the boat into a zawn (Cornish for a narrow inlet) alongside a suitable ledge, and one had to judge the right moment on an upward surge to leap out with the coiled bow-rope. A firm stance had to be taken up quickly to hold the strong pull of a full boat in the backwash. Whenever it was an officer the men secretly hoped that he would be dragged in, but they had to be content with us getting soaked with spray as we held the boat for each man to jump in turn. With sea all around there was no option but to climb the cliff after we had landed.

The Cornish people were friendly, and the fishermen in the pubs in Sennen and St Ives had plenty of anecdotes to tell. Their wives sat outside on a sunny day knitting the string vests which were issued to us Commandos. These were a great improvement on soaking shirts which dried on us after our exertions, for the loose stitching of the thick white string trapped air which kept us warmer than clammy cloth. (Later nylon imitations I treated with disdain, and I used my string vests on my post-war expeditions to Norway, Iceland and Greenland, and to Everest Base Camp. On a Sandhurst exercise in Brittany I was tickled pink to come across a genuine string vest on display in a war museum com-memorating the Resistance, where Special Forces had given assistance.)

The training on the cliffs came into immediate use as, leaving my window ajar, I climbed up to my room when the front door was locked by the time that I had walked back to Carbis Bay from the pubs in St Ives. The bill has survived – it cost £4. 1s. for nine days at the Chy-an-Drea Hotel in 1944.

When I got back to Scotland Charlie Vaughan told me, rather to my relief, that he would not be needing me. He must have realised that, so fresh out of OCTU, I was really too young. After the months in huts it was a strange experience to spend a night in the officers' mess in the house itself, and briefly to be on equal terms with the instructors.

Back I went to Gibraltar Camp. On the morning of 6 June we were in the ablution hut when someone who had been listening to the wireless came in and announced that the D-Day invasion had started. We looked at one another, and it certainly went through my mind that we would be the cannon-fodder replacements for the casualties.

The last stage in this direction was a posting to the Holding Operational Commando (HOC) in a barracks at Wrexham. This was a difficult place for the Directing Staff to run, as batches were continuously being posted in and out for varying periods, and a training programme had to be organised to keep them occupied. Captain Dennis O'Flaherty had been appointed Adjutant, and he decided to tighten up on discipline. As a subaltern in 3 Commando he had won a DSO in the raid on Vaagso in December 1941. After storming into a warehouse he received a bullet at close range in the eye which came out through the back of his neck. Despite this he managed to walk out again, and was taken back to the ship. The damage was too severe for an artificial eye to be fitted so he had to wear a black patch, and it was rumoured that his head was held on by wire. This legendary figure was a complete martinet, and put the fear of God into us young officers. One day I walked into the officers' ante-room in Old College at the Academy and instantly recognised a small figure at the bar, even though his back was towards me. Sure enough, when he turned round there was the black patch, and I tentatively introduced myself. When I got to know him well I discovered that he was a warm and human person, and we became good friends. At Wrexham he had been the unapproachable Adjutant, but fourteen years later the three-years' difference in age was of no account.

His Troop Commander at Vaagso had been Peter Young. When 43 RM Commando was disbanded after our return from Italy I was posted to 46 RM Commando. Brigadier Peter Young was our overall commander, and I remember the occasion on which he came to inspect us. The Brigade was due to follow up Operation 'Zipper', the invasion of Malaya, and the story was that we were scheduled to attack an officer training centre; so it was as well that the atom bombs brought about the Japanese surrender, as they would have been a bit too keen to fight to the last man. When he retired from the Army, Peter Young came to the Academy as head of the Military History department. As an extra-mural activity for the cadets he started the Sealed Knot Civil War society, which he later developed on a national scale, re-enacting battles with contemporary dress and weapons all over the country.

Above: Zivio Drug Tito – Long Live Comrade Tito. ...rsigia, one of the many female Partisans on Vis, is ...spected prior to guard duty. (IWM NA.18271)
...low: The British Mission organised an increasing flow ...arms and equipment, including battledress, to the Partisans. These messenger boys are well equipped with captured German weapons, *patronentaschen* (ammunition pouches), and *feldflasche mit trinkbecher* (waterbottle and mug). (IWM NA.18280)

Left: Portrait of a commissar; twenty-seven-year-old Baca. (IWM NA.18224)

Below: Vis harbour, a quiet spot before the war, was a hive of activi* in 1944. (IWM NA.18248)

Above: Singing their rousing song 'Dalmatinska', Partisans based on Vis embark on a schooner captured from the Germans for an operation on Korcula Island, 2 August 1944. (IWM NA.18228)

Below: This panorama was taken by a member of No. 2 Army Photographic Unit which was permanently based with the British forces supporting the Partisans on Vis. (IWM NA.18249)

Above: A Partisan on the Korcula raid is festooned with an ammunition belt for his German MG42 light machine-gun, and with British hand-grenades. He carries a fannion for one of the battalions of I Brigade, part of the Partisan XXVI Division based on Vis. (IWM NA.18225)

Opposite page, top: RCLs (Ramped Cargo Lighters) of the Royal Navy land 25-pounders of F Troop, 476 Battery, III Field Regiment, RA at Loviste on the Peljesac peninsula, 27 August 1944. The 'artillery raid' was code named 'Grandfather 1'. (IWM NA.18102)

Opposite page, bottom: Two 25-pounders of F Troop firing on the positions of II/750 Jaeger Regiment and its supporting artillery at Pupnat on Korcula Island across the Peljesacki Channel during 'Grandfather 1'. (IWM NA.18096)

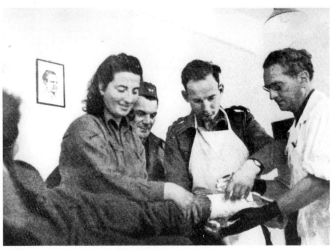

Left: Captain McWilliams, MO of 2 Commando, treating a wounded female Partisan.

Centre left: E Troop with a Partisan flag.

Below: General Draza Mihailovic (next to musician), a pre-war regular officer who organised the Royalist Serb Cetniks.

Opposite page: Josip Broz, 'Tito', Croat Communist leader of the Partisans. He is wearing the Marshal's uniform recently presented to him by the Russians, 14 May 1944. (IWM NA.15732)

Above: Marshal Tito reviewing 2 Commando on Vis with Brigadier Tom Churchill, 2 August 1944. (IWM NA CNA.3744)

Below: E Troop at Putignano, Italy, October 1944. Marine Alick Maclean is second from the left, second row from the front.

43
ROYAL   MARINE
COMMANDO

One morning at Wrexham when I was at a loose end I wandered into the office of the Troop commander, Captain Peter Haydon, and inquired if there was anything to do. (Haydon had won a DSO as a young lieutenant at Salerno. After recovering from his wounds he rejoined 41 RM Commando, but sadly he was to be killed at Walcheren.) He looked at his training programme and said that two groups were practising river crossings about ten miles west in the Llantysilio area, which I could watch. I made my way there and tracked down the first group, who were doing leopard-crawl across. A horizontal rope is slung between two trees on either bank and the procedure is to climb up, lie on top, hook one foot around the rope and leave the other leg dangling for balance. Then it is a matter of combining a pull with the arms with a push from the ankle; straightforward for the majority, but not for the few with a fear of water. In a training establishment early on in a course it is not possible to know each man's strengths and weaknesses as one does in a unit.

Everything was going smoothly until I noticed that one man was making slow progress. Half-way across he lost his balance, and was left hanging by his arms. Again there are standard drills. After pulling up with the arms, one hooks a leg over the rope to relieve the weight. Then either the other leg can be hooked over so as to pull across underneath the rope, or one can give a pendulum swing with the free leg to get on top in the leopard position again. This man failed to get his leg back over, and in the end he dropped off. I thought to myself that after a wetting he would improve his technique next time. But instead of swimming to the bank he started flailing about, and then went under. All of a sudden I realised that he must be a weak swimmer, so I shouted to the sergeant in charge, the only person I knew there, to get the safety boat out. To my dismay he said that it was farther upstream with the other group, so we dispatched someone at the double to fetch it. Meanwhile two Marines on the bank had spotted that their comrade was in trouble, and had quickly stripped off. There were two safety ropes, and we tied them round their waists. The man came up a second time in the same place, but waved his arms about again, and sank once more. Everyone does a basic test in a swimming bath, but for a weak swimmer it must be very difficult to get going with boots and denims on. The third time he came up one of the Marines got to him, but tragically he struggled so frantically that it prevented his rescuer from getting hold of him, and we were appalled to see him disappear yet again. The Marines duck-dived to try to find him until they were exhausted, and we had to haul them in. The safety boat arrived shortly afterwards, but it proved impossible to locate him, and the body was recovered several hours later farther downstream. The river was not more than twelve yards wide, and on this flat stretch there was little current. I had to attend the Coroner's Inquiry, where he gave a verdict of Accidental Death, with a commendation to the two Marines for their rescue attempt.

When I was on embarkation leave shortly afterwards I told my parents all about it. The coffin had been sent to the soldier's home by rail, and I had heard that for a while it had gone astray. I joked that the corpse had not been able to rectify matters – only because the man was completely unknown to me. My father remarked in a relieved voice that the incident had not affected me too badly. He had enlisted after his first term at Aberystwith University at the end of 1914 and his first encounter with death had been a great deal closer and more personal. His regiment was waiting in the front line for another unit to relieve them. In the Cuinchy sector the opposing trenches were very close, and snipers were able to take up positions on brick-stacks. A friend of his was standing a few feet away with his back to a right-angled traverse in the trench. Feeling relaxed after completing another stint, he lit a cigarette. Moments later he was lying at my father's feet with a bullet-hole through his forehead.

I marvel at the fortitude of that generation. True, as with us, there was nothing for it but to continue with what the higher command required, but it must have been soul-destroying to go back time and time and time again carrying heavy loads and subject to cold, rain, sticky mud, hard-tack rations, rats, snipers' bullets, machine-gun bursts, rifle-grenades, exploding shells, dangerous patrols and suicidal attacks. The chances of arbitrary death were much higher than in our more mobile actions and shorter spells of danger. Moreover they had to contend with gas as well. My uncle Llewellyn lost most of his hair, the rest turned white, and his lungs were permanently weakened. After the winter of 1915–16 my father got severe rheumatism in his hip until eventually he was unable to march. This probably saved his life, as he was invalided home just before the battle of the Somme. It appals yet fascinates me that men continued to move forward into such senseless slaughter after the carefully planned artillery bombardment failed to achieve its purpose. My father still had a conscience that he was not there with his comrades.

His treatment took some time, but the joint remained stiff, so as a volunteer he was able to get a discharge from the army. He re-enlisted in the Royal Flying Corps as he managed to persuade the medical authorities that his handicap would not prevent him from flying. Again it was fortunate that the armistice was signed before he completed his training, as life expectancy for novice pilots was not long.

At HOC 'milling' came more to the fore, to keep us 'tough'. In this you are roughly matched up, and the aim is to belt your opponent as often as possible for three minutes, with little regard for the niceties of boxing. If a man is knocked down he is hauled out of the ring by his heels, and the next pair set to straight away. There was a group of South Africans at Wrexham who had seconded to the Marines, and Joffre Britz was my height and weight. The difference was that he was a very good amateur boxer, whereas I had done little. By keeping on the attack I was able to put him off his stroke for a while, but then he would get in the old one-two – a left to the face to bring my arms up, and then a thumping right to the solar plexus which made me gasp. On one occasion I was matched with a chap who was much bigger than myself, and early on I landed a punch that made his nose bleed. The blood collected on his bushy fair moustache, my gloves daubed it further over his face, and I was pleased that it looked as if I was doing well, although in fact he was not badly hurt.

The year's training had put me in very good stead. I was the first to leave for active service – to the Mediterranean, whereas the other five joined Commandos which fought across north-west Europe. A batch of us flew out at the beginning of August 1944, so it was a rapid transition to hotter conditions. On the way we staged at Gibraltar, where the airstrip runs across the narrow causeway. As we came down under the shadow of the Rock and sped along the runway I suddenly became concerned that the brakes might not work, as the plane was heading for open sea at the far end.

The next leg was to Bari in southern Italy, where we had to hang about for a couple of days before joining 43 RM Commando on the Yugoslav island of Vis. When I went to rear HQ at Molfetta the very first Marine whom I met in a theatre of war was rolling drunk, with a bottle of vino in his hand. His cheery greeting of 'Hello Tosh' was not quite what I expected, but I decided that it was best to ignore the matter.

CHAPTER 3

Operations on the Dalmatian Islands

A major battle had been fought on the island of Brac and nine of us landed on Vis on 9 August 1944 to join 43 RM Commando to make up numbers.

Two CS (Continuous Service *ie* Regular) Captains, Ian Gourlay and Ralph Parkinson-Cumine, had served in Marine detachments on 'big ships' before coming ashore for Commando training. The two friends were quiet, assured, intelligent men of the highest calibre. Ian was promoted to full General when he became Commandant General of the Marines, and in my opinion PC would undoubtedly have succeeded him in this appointment had he not been killed in Korea. Of the subalterns three were mature South Africans – Martin Preston, who later became a Troop Commander, 'Shorty' Venter and Joffre Britz; and among the rest of us Don Esson later became Adjutant, Mike McConville was a wild Irishman, Nick Demuth a good musician, and the ninth was myself.

When the 'Jug' schooner tied up at the quay, a friendly officer met us with some transport and drove us up the winding road to the west, where 43 RM Commando was under canvas and in bivouacs on the hillsides. In August this was enjoyable, and officers were provided with camp beds, but living out in the open had been a different story during severe weather in February and March. During my stay I walked out to the two small forts at the entrance to Vis harbour. They were in fact built by the British when a naval squadron was based on the island during the Napoleonic Wars, and the eastern one is named Velington. The Navy won an encounter with the French off Vis in 1811.

PC and I took over E Troop. I was particularly fortunate to have him as my Troop Commander: his steady and wise guidance was invaluable. The establishment was for two subalterns, but we were never up to strength on men, so the two of us worked together all the way through. It became standard routine to get up at six o'clock, put on socks, boots and shorts, and to double down a steep zig-zag track to the sea to have a swim. The quick march back up kept us fit, before we had breakfast. This did not vary much on compo rations, and we had hard-tack Army biscuits morning, noon and night, which became very monotonous. Very occasionally we managed to barter for some loaves with the Partisans, which we savoured to the full, and equally rarely our amateur cook, McMasters, somehow got hold of some flour and baked dampers in biscuit tin

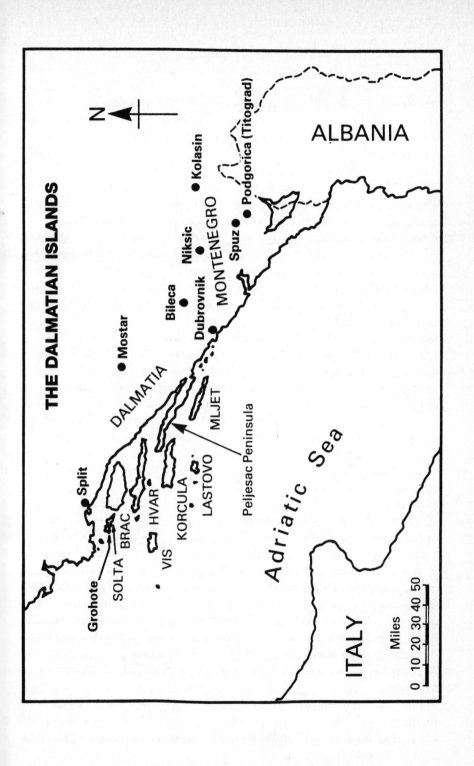

THE DALMATIAN ISLANDS

N

ALBANIA

Podgorica (Titograd)

Kolasin

Niksic

Spuz

MONTENEGRO

Bileca

Dubrovnik

Mostar

DALMATIA

MLJET

Peljesac Peninsula

Split

Adriatic Sea

Grohote

SOLTA

BRAC

VIS

HVAR

KORCULA

LASTOVO

ITALY

Miles

0 10 20 30 40 50

ovens, which were much appreciated – shades of Boy Scout days! Normally he used a roaring field cooker, but when this broke down we improvised with jerry cans. Sand was fed in to fill about three inches at the bottom, and soaked with petrol. Two small holes were punched into the narrow side of the can just above. A lighted match was dropped in, the cap was firmly secured, and when pressure had built up the jets from the holes were lit. One evening a Marine (no names, no pack-drill) was doing this close to my tent, and I was idly watching. He dropped in the match, but only half-secured the cap, so that flames belched out. To my astonishment he just dumped the can and legged it. There was the danger of the tent being burnt or of an explosion so I scrambled out, grabbed the handle and hurled the can clear. I was not best pleased.

Each week a highlight was the issue of NAAFI duty-free drink, cigarettes, chocolate and soap. Money was meaningless in Yugoslavia at that time. This saved me from smoking, as I had never inhaled, so I kept mine for bartering, or gave them to some of the men if they got too desperate. We acquired a small wine barrel which we refilled in Komiza with the tasty local red prusac wine, in exchange for tins of compo. The cellar there had enormous barrels about nine feet high, so it involved clambering up on a ladder with a length of thick rubber hose and giving a great suck to bring the wine down by gravity. Grapes were beginning to ripen, and provided us with fresh fruit.

Knowing PC, we must have kept up our training, but I only remember one incident. There was a hollow where it was safe for pistol practice, so several of us were firing at tins with our Colt 45s. I was not much good, but a young signaller, Wolstenholme, was able to keep a tin on the move. In praising his skill I used his nickname. PC brought the matter up in the tent that evening, and pointed out that it was a fine line on retaining respect if one became too familiar. Since then I have always stuck to surnames.

Relations with the Partisans on Vis were very friendly. There is no doubt that Tito had enthusiastic support from all his followers, whether Communist or not. 'Zivio Tito' ('Long Live Tito') was painted on walls everywhere, and we found the same thing on the mainland later on. 'Smrt Fasismu' ('Death to Fascism') was another of their slogans. Their hardships had fashioned a puritanical discipline. Those found guilty of looting or sexual misconduct were shot, women as well, so there was no feminine comfort in our Spartan life. A quarter of Tito's forces were women. They had equal status, suffered the same hardships in winter living 'in sume' (in the woods), and frequently took part in the fighting. After their merciless treatment at the hands of the Germans the Partisans had a nasty habit of shooting prisoners, which we did our best to try to prevent.

Their own uniform consisted of a grey-green serge jacket and trousers with leather belt and braces and wellington-type boots, but many were dressed in captured German and Italian uniforms. British boots and battledress were just beginning to appear. All of them, men and women, festooned themselves with a formidable array of pistols, hand-grenades and bandoliers of ammunition of every conceivable type. Although good at ambushes and quick withdrawal, they were not well trained in using covering fire for formal attacks such as on Brac, and they often suffered heavy casualties from brave frontal assaults. The three medical officers with the Commandos treated as many wounded Partisans as they could.

To improve their marksmanship the Partisans simply selected a target and got on with it. Several times when I was walking along tracks on the hillsides there was the sharp crack of a bullet that had passed mighty close. My third encounter with 'friendly' fire. I looked hard for the culprits, but they kept still and were concealed, so their fieldcraft was better than their safety precautions.

We picked up a smattering of Serbo-Croat – key words to help us get along. In all matters, protocol was respected. One directive that I was nominated to deal with ran as follows:

From Adm. HQ VIS Bde. Enclosed please find the following tickets:
Sjedalo parter (Seats downstairs) – 8
Stajanje parter (Standing downstairs) – 8
Stajanje galerija (Standing gallery) – 12
The tickets read:
KAZALIŠTE NARODNOG OSLOBODENJA
Narodni Dom-Vis
_____

ULAZNICA
Sjedalo parter
Broj: 100   Red: VIII
I-IX 1944   Početak u 18-30
The stamp had a red star in the centre, encircled by
OKROZNI N.O.O.
Srednie Dalmatinskog Otocja

Each ticket enables one person to enter the Yugo-Slav National Theatre at VIS to an entertainment given by the Partisan Army at 1830 hrs on 1 Sep. 44.

As these tickets are issued at the request of the Supreme HQ of the Yugo-Slav National Army of Liberation it is hoped that in the interests of good relationship with the Partisans all will be used.

Indecipherably signed. DAA & QMG
20 Beach Gp.

I do not know how many of my party had to be pressed men, but it made a change.

The Partisans along the coast were ebullient, and it was mainly through singing that we established cameraderie. We mastered their rousing Brigade song 'Dalmatinska' and enjoyed the melodic tunes of their traditional Dalmatian airs. They in their turn did their best to get hold of 'Tipperary'. These get-togethers were swept along by the local firebrand drink, rakija, but the Partisan code was severe on drunkenness, so no one went too far. The only time that I ever saw PC put out was at one of these gatherings. A pretty little Partisan girl started playing dangerously with her pistol, and every time it pointed in his direction PC looked distinctly uneasy and shifted his position. I was highly amused, but he knew how easily stupid accidents can occur.

With two safe harbours, Vis suited the Navy well. Lieutenant-Commander Morgan-Giles built up a fast, hard-hitting force of MTBs (motor torpedo boats) and MGBs (motor gun goats) to disrupt German sea traffic. Commandos provided small boarding parties, and although on most patrols they did not come across suitable targets, there were some successes. A seven-man party from 43 RM Commando led by Lieutenant D.B. Clark boarded five lighters in succession. They were towed back to Komiza, and the cargoes included tons of Danish butter and flour. The Marines in E Troop were still talking about the welcome change from dry biscuits. Large LCIs (landing craft infantry) and smaller LCAs (landing craft assault) were concealed under camouflage netting around the coast of Vis to provide amphibious transport for Commando recces and raids. When 111 Field Regiment RA first joined the garrison they had to improvise by taking off the wheels from their 25-pounders in order to get them into LCAs. Later larger LCTs (landing craft tank) arrived, and the guns could be driven on and off over the ramp at the bow. The Navy's tally during 1943–4 was one destroyer and eighty-four smaller craft sunk, twenty-four captured and thirteen damaged.

After a great deal of hard work by the Partisans under the expert supervision of Royal Engineers an airstrip was constructed in Plisko Polje, just south of the road below Podselje, which enabled Spitfires and Hurricanes to extend their operations over the mainland. Most of Vis is formed of craggy, steep-sided hills, as the islands are remnants of former mountain ranges which were drowned after the Ice Ages. Inland in the southern half there is a flatter polje (limestone solution basin), and the vineyards, olive groves and stone walls were levelled. When the United States Army Airforce stepped up its raids on the Ploesti oilfields in Romania, the strip was extended as far as possible until the limit was reached by a hill at one end and a drop at the other. Damaged Liberators and Flying Fortresses made emergency landings, but they were hazardous. Often the crews baled out over the island, and the pilot alone brought the plane in, or it was allowed to crash into the sea. The airstrip was about three miles east of E Troop lines, and sometimes when the crews jumped out too high when a strong wind was blowing we watched them being carried inexorably out to sea. The Navy did their best to pick them up. There were

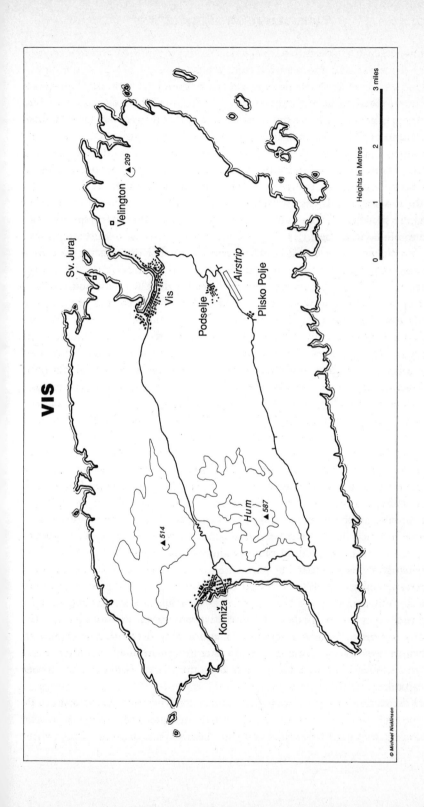

VIS

Sv. Juraj

Velington

▲ 209

Vis

Podselje

Airstrip

Plisko Polje

▲ 514

Hum

▲ 587

Komiža

Heights in Metres

0   1   2   3 miles

© Michael Nickinson

215 emergency landings, and altogether, including the parachutists, almost 2000 British and American airmen were saved.

One American crew was not so lucky. One morning a particularly loud roar of engines brought us out of our tents. A struggling Liberator just cleared the ridge opposite, but as it banked eastwards a wing hit the ground and it crashed. I yelled to our First Aid man to bring his pack, and we rushed down the slope and up the other side. We got all the crew out, but they were badly smashed up. Only one man was breathing stertorously and he was unconscious. I sent two men back to get a stretcher, and told the signallers to report the situation to the hospital and to Garrison HQ. (In the Marines we trained our First Aid staff and signallers. Cooks, however, were volunteers and in that respect we just had to hope for the best.) There was a razor-sharp two-edged knife strapped to the leg of one of the bodies which I removed to slice through the parachute harness of the survivor in order to check on his injuries. After the sudden shock of impact no blood was coming from his deep wounds, and the only thing that we could do was to try to keep him warm. We carried him across to the nearest point on a road where he was taken off in a vehicle, but I had little hope for his chances. In checking round the aircraft I came across an escape pack. It contained a silk scarf printed with a map of the Balkans, some currency, a small compass and concentrated rations. Eventually an officer from HQ turned up who knew how to deal with the situation, so I told him what had happened, and handed over the pack to him. He gave me the rations, which would be useful on operations.

*   *   *

A brief resumé of the military situation may be helpful at this point. The first external Fascist threat to Yugoslavia came when Mussolini occupied Albania in April 1939, as a move to re-establish former Roman and Venetian control over the Adriatic. In the spring of 1941 Hitler decided to secure his southern flank before he attacked the Soviet Union, so he subjected Prince Paul, the Regent of Yugoslavia, to strong political pressure and threats. On 24 March Prince Paul reluctantly signed a neutrality pact with the Axis. Three days later military officers staged a *coup d'état*, replaced Paul by the young King Peter and, with popular support, renounced the pact. Hitler's reaction was swift. On 6 April he ruthlessly bombed Belgrade and launched twenty-seven divisions against the poorly organised Yugoslav forces. His intention was to subdue Greece as well, which Mussolini had been unable to do after his unilateral attack on the country in October 1940. The blitzkrieg lasted eleven days. Yugoslavia was forced to capitulate.

Hitler's aim was to conserve his own troops for Operation 'Barbarossa', so he allowed Mussolini to garrison Dalmatia, Montenegro and Kosovo. Cynically exploiting internal divisions, he set up the Fascist state of Croatia, which included Bosnia and Herzegovina, and he appointed Ante Pavelic as dictator. Fanatical Croat nationalists, the Ustase, inflicted terrible atrocities against the long-established Serb and Muslim communities within the new state.

Two Resistance groups emerged. The Cetniks, led by Colonel Draza Mihailovic, were Royalist and strongly Serbian nationalist. A radio monitoring station at Portishead picked up messages from Mihailovic in August 1941, and the Cetniks were recognised by King Peter and his government-in-exile. In September 1941 Captain D.T. Hudson, working for Special Operations Executive, was landed from a submarine in the Gulf of Kotor to provide a link with Mihailovic at his HQ in Serbia. He soon received help from anti-Italian guerrillas, but they were not Cetniks. At their HQ at Radovce he discovered that they had been organised by Milovan Djilas, an ardent Communist. Djilas provided him with horses, and he had a brief meeting with the main leader, 'Tito', on his way to the Cetnik HQ at Ravna Gora. For eighteen months Hudson was the only liaison officer in Yugoslavia, and the meagre military supplies that could be spared from Allied commitments in North Africa were sent to the Cetniks.

As a professional soldier Mihailovic fully appreciated the military odds against him, and his policy was to husband his resources until the tide began to turn. He considered that the limited damage that he could inflict by sabotage operations did not justify the savage reprisals which the Germans took against the civilian population.

Tito was much more resolute, and less parochial. His aim was to free the whole of Yugoslavia from Axis occupation. As a Marxist, the end justified the means, so he was prepared to attack, despite the sacrifices and hardship. He emphasised a Popular Front, and his slogan, which appealed to the Slavs' innate desire for freedom, was 'Sloboda Narodu' – 'Liberty to the People'. Volunteers from all parts of the country and from all walks of life joined the Partisans. Most of them were not Communist, but hard-core cadres of Party members had firm control over the movement. Every Partisan wore a five-pointed Red Star in his or her forage cap.

Not until Germany broke the Nazi–Soviet pact of 1939 by invading the Soviet Union on 22 June 1941 did Tito commit his Partisan organisation to fighting the occupying powers. He had two brief meetings with Mihailovic to see if joint action could be arranged, but little was achieved, as their political differences were too profound. Mihailovic and his followers detested Communism even more than they did the Fascists (except for the Ustase). Evidence emerged that ill-disciplined Cetnik leaders collaborated with the Italians and Germans in order to attack the Partisans. During the occupation there was a bitter civil war – Cetniks, Partisans and Ustase ruthlessly killed one another.

The Axis forces used their armour, artillery and air power to mount numerous offensives against the Partisans. In May 1943 Captain Bill Deakin was parachuted into Montenegro with a wireless team to make the first direct official contact with Tito. He arrived at the start of the Fifth offensive, and for two months suffered all the hardships as the Partisans were constantly harried. A German body-count afterwards recorded that 5697 Partisan men and women were killed, over 2500 civilians were shot, and fifty villages were burned down. About 10,000 Partisans managed to break out from encirclement, and made their weary way to central Bosnia. Deakin signalled back that he was much impressed by Tito's leadership, and by the resilience and fighting qualities of his forces. He recommended that a senior officer should be sent out.

Marshal Badoglio's capitulation on 8 September 1943 took everyone in Yugoslavia by surprise, including the Germans. Tito's Partisans were the first to get to the Italian garrisons, and the large quantities of arms, vehicles and equipment which they acquired gave a great boost to their fortunes. Some Italian units agreed to change sides, and Tito used them in support roles. The Germans sent in strong armoured and motorised columns with air support to regain control of the Yugoslav mainland. Reoccupation of the Dalmatian islands required amphibious operations, and took longer, but German garrisons had been established on all the islands except for Vis by the middle of January 1944. Vis, eleven miles by five, and lying about twenty-seven miles out from Split, was the best remaining potential base for providing assistance to the Partisans.

Churchill personally appointed Fitzroy Maclean to be head of a British Mission to Tito and he was promptly promoted to Brigadier. Prior to the war he had been a diplomat in Russia, which was a reserved occupation. In order to be free to join up he got himself elected as a Conservative MP in a by-election, after which he promptly resigned. It was not long before he was engaged in Special Air Service operations in the Middle East. After hand-picking his staff he parachuted in to Tito's HQ at Jajce in September 1943, nine days after the Italian surrender. His reports confirmed that the Partisans were well led and organised, and that it was their attacking spirit which was forcing Germany to keep so many troops in the country. On the political side he stressed that Tito had close ties with Moscow. Churchill was influenced more by the strategic practicalities, and in December 1943 Britain switched military support from the less effective Mihailovic to the more aggressive Tito.

This was reflected in one of the policy statements after the conference between the Big Three at Teheran. They agreed: 'That the Partisans in Yugoslavia should be supported by supplies and equipment to the greatest possible extent, and also by Commando operations'.

Maclean recruited Major Randolph Churchill, Winston's son, as a member of his staff. Randolph had served with the Commandos, and he introduced Maclean to Brigadier Tom Churchill, the commander of 2 Special Service Brigade, who was most interested in a Commando role on Vis. Maclean then put his proposals for securing Vis as a base personally to General Alexander and to the Prime Minister, and obtained their endorsement. Faced with the imminent threat of a German landing, Tito and the local Partisan naval and military commanders readily agreed to joint British/Partisan defence of the island.

On 16 January the advance party of 2 Commando landed on Vis, to be followed soon afterwards by the rest of the unit, depleted in numbers after their action at Salerno. 43 RM Commando, which had taken part in the Anzio landings and had been fighting on the River Garigliano front, moved across in cattle trucks to Bari and embarked to join 2 Commando at the end of February. German naval records show that Operation 'Freischutz' for the occupation of Vis was planned but, probably because of the British presence, it was not implemented. They did carry out a bombing attack on 28 March. A 500-pounder scored a direct hit on the only building allocated to 43 RM Commando for occupation, killing an officer and two signallers, and destroying many of the HQ records. 40 RM Commando arrived on Vis on 5 May, so Green Berets were thick on the ground. By the time that the nine of us arrived in August a wide variety of other units had been added, so, with the First Dalmatian Partisan Brigade sharing the island with us, there was plenty of activity.

The CO of 2 Commando was Lieutenant Colonel Jack Churchill, elder brother of Brigadier Tom. 'Mad Jack' was a colourful character, renowned for his playing of the bagpipes and his wielding of a claymore in action. The immediate priority was deployment for the defence of the island, but this done he turned his attention to a role closer to his heart – raids on the enemy. There was a great deal of small-scale activity – recce parties liaised with the Partisans on the other islands to observe the movements of the German garrisons. Captain Bare took his Troop across to Hvar to attack a strongpoint. Four Germans were killed and four wounded, but Bare himself was killed leading the assault. He was buried with full military honours in the small British naval cemetery just outside Vis town. Nearby was the weathered tombstone of the Honourable Richard Anson, killed in action on his frigate in 1811. During the cold conditions in February, Lieutenant Barton was roaming around Brac with a ten-man party, and the local Partisans helped him to acquire a great deal of detailed intelligence. So much so that he decided to target the German Commandant who had begun to impose severe measures on the civilian population. He concealed a Sten-gun in a firewood-bundle loaded on a mule which a woman led, as prearranged, to a barn in the village of Nerezisce, the main German base. One evening Barton disguised himself as a shepherd, and got past the sentries by joining a couple of locals when they routinely drove their sheep back into the village. When darkness fell he retrieved his Sten, discarded the cloak and trousers he had worn over his uniform, and made his way

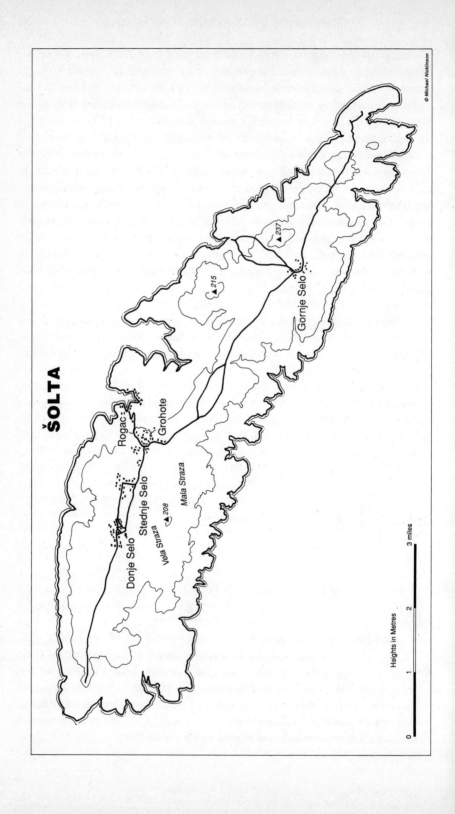

ŠOLTA

Rogac

Grohote

Stednje Selo

Donje Selo

Vela Straza

Mala Straza

▲ 208

Gornje Selo

▲ 215

▲ 237

© Michael Nicklinson

Heights in Metres

0   1   2   3 miles

to the Commandant's house. Fortunately for him the batmen were absent; he located his victim in the dining room, gave him two lethal bursts and managed to escape. A boat was sent to bring him and his party back the next day to Vis.

Comprehensive reconnaissance reports from Solta enabled Lieutenant Colonel Churchill to mount a full Commando attack on 18 March 1944. 43 RM Commando was in position to safeguard Vis, and Churchill took their Vickers Section to increase the support fire from his own Heavy Weapons Troop. It was a well-planned combined operation. Two LCIs, each towing an LCA, put the party ashore shortly after midnight. Guides led each Troop to previously selected positions, and before dawn the Commando was surrounding the German garrison in the village of Grohote. All the weapons and ammunition had to be man-packed, so the approach march with heavy loads over the steep hillsides was exhausting. The key to success was an RAF bombing attack at 0600. Stan Buckmaster, a redoubtable Bren-gunner, has given this vivid description:

Using a Loud Hailer Lt Col Jack Churchill called upon the garrison to give up and surrender; he also informed them that they were about to be bombed unless they did so. As this demand was being made through an interpreter, thirty-six Kitty Hawks arrived over the town. They flew in low at the start, over the roof-tops, before they swept upwards to form a 'Cab rank'. Then, taking directions from a ground control officer who was with the colonel, they peeled off into a steep dive a dozen at a time. As the dive commenced they opened fire with their 20 mm cannon and machine guns, which were firing tracer, and at the point where they flattened out, released their bombs. From below it appeared as though they were descending on golden rails, the unbroken lines of tracer giving this effect. The assault Troop fixed bayonets, and as the last wave of aircraft dived down over the target, they dashed into the main street and commenced clearing the houses of the enemy. This part of the plan was a master stroke, as these planes were firing blank ammunition, allowing the Commandos to move in under a curtain of noise rather than fire, whilst the Germans had their 'heads down'.

During the attack those of us immediately below the flight path of the aircraft were showered with the spent cannon shells and machine-gun cartridge castings as they fell away from the planes. We had been informed that this was likely, and were warned to wear our steel helmets to avoid injury.

Among the early captives during the street fighting was the German garrison Commandant. He was brought to where Colonel Churchill had made his surrender demand, and in turn called upon his men to stop fighting. He was able to assure them that the attacking force was British, and that they would be treated correctly as PoW under the terms of the Geneva Convention. Partisans were apt to give their prisoners short shrift, largely as a result of the manner in which they themselves had been treated by the enemy.

Gradually the firing died away, as various sections of the defenders were rounded up, disarmed and made prisoner. Many civilians had made a mass exodus from the town whilst the fighting was actually going on. We had no idea as to the extent of casualties among them, although there must have been some, as many houses had been destroyed or damaged during the bombing. Among the prisoners were several Ustase, and local collaborators. A thorough search of the town ensured that all the garrison were in the net. Eventually all was ready to return to the beach, and the prisoners were lined up, some being detailed to assist with carrying the heavy equipment. Col. Jack Churchill took his place at the head of the column and we marched away from Grohote to the tune of 'Road to the Isles' played by the Colonel on his bagpipes. We had lost two men killed and had several wounded, but had captured over a hundred prisoners, and they had lost at least eight dead and many wounded.

It turned out that the civilian casualties were limited to four killed and two wounded, so it was a most successful operation. The Germans regarrisoned with a larger force of 250 men. They built strong positions protected by mines and wire, from which they repulsed two later attacks by the First Dalmatian Brigade. On the second occasion the Partisans evacuated the civilian population in case of reprisals. On 17 September 1944 I took part in the final operation, mounted by 43 RM Commando, which, thanks to the Navy this time, ended with the final elimination of Germans from the island.

The first joint operation, involving most of 43 RM Commando, 280 men, and two Battalions of the Dalmatian Brigade, about 400 in all, landed on Hvar on 22 March 1944 to destroy the German garrison at Jelsa, estimated to be around 200 strong. Lieutenant Colonel 'Bonzo' Simonds (CO 43) was the Force Commander; Major Neil Munro (2 i/c) took command of 43 RM Commando; and Bogdan, a cheerful man with a fierce black moustache, led the Partisans. 43 RM Commando left Vis harbour in an LCI: the Partisans were in five schooners; and as it was a daylight crossing the Navy provided an escort of a MTB and a couple of mine-sweepers. The Commandos landed before last light on the south coast, but the schooners did not arrive until three hours later, and the Partisans disembarked farther east. Resident recce parties reported that after the prearranged RAF bombing attack in the afternoon the garrison had shown signs of moving out. The advance Troops of 43 RM Commando set off quickly to climb the central ridge and surround Jelsa. In the darkness a German column heading eastward from the town blundered into the rear Troop, commanded by Captain 'Jock' Hudspith. There was a fierce fire-fight. Although the Marines were outnumbered, the Germans broke off the engagement and continued to head east, leaving behind five dead, four prisoners, and their mule-train loaded with wireless equipment, ammunition and personal baggage. Next they ran into the Partisans, and bloodier hand-to-hand fighting ensued. Ten Germans were killed and thirty captured. The remnants turned back towards Jelsa, only to encounter A Troop again. Six more were killed and two taken prisoner. Two Marines were wounded in this second clash. By morning it had become a hunt. The 3-inch mortar section, after a strenuous carry of their equipment and bombs for several miles, at last observed a group of Germans resting bunched together. An accurate shoot killed fifteen of them. The final outcome was fifty Germans killed and eighty captured. Seventeen Italians caught up in the affair had given themselves up promptly. The Partisans lost four killed, one of whom was a woman, and fourteen were wounded.

In his report, Lieutenant Colonel Simonds was full of praise for the Partisans' fighting spirit, but he commented on their impetuosity and poor fire control. In a battle they were liable to fire at anything that moved, whether British or German, and they opened up regardless of range. After this combined action 43 RM Commando HQ received a letter from Partisan Brigade HQ addressed 'To our Comrades in the Fight Against the German Barbars'. The Barbars re-established a garrison on Hvar.

On Vis 43 RM Commando practised coordinated two-Troop attacks through dummy minefields and wire, as the Germans were busy putting added protection around their fortified bunkers. On 1 May 1944 there was another enemy air attack and 43 HQ, now in a new location, again became a target. Sixteen bombs destroyed some precious transport but this time there were no casualties, as slit trenches provided protection. 40 RM Commando arrived shortly after this raid, and used a bomb crater as an easy site in which to dig latrines – until it was pointed out to them that that particular crater had been formed by an unexploded bomb!

On 22 May 1944 a strong foray on to Mljet by 2 Commando and 43 RM Commando, plus a Troop from 40 RM Commando, was unsuccessful. It turned into the most exhausting test of endurance that the men had ever experienced, and all to no avail. Bad weather delayed the crossing for two days; the objectives required too much to be attempted in too short a time; and their execution was thwarted when reinforcements were sent across quickly. Mjlet has the steepest ridges in the archipelago, and for once the Partisan guides left the tracks, so the heavily laden men literally had to bash their way through thick, tangled scrub. Major Munro reached his start-line five hours late, and Captain Blake took even longer to get to his. By the time they had climbed to their first assigned hilltops they found that the Germans had withdrawn to concentrate in their defences on the north coast. At their first objectives, 2 Commando found that the same thing had happened. Mljet lies close to the mainland, so big guns were able to bring down defensive fire to protect the formidable northern strongpoints. Brigadier Churchill was not prepared to incur heavy casualties. He ordered a withdrawal back to the LCIs on the south coast.

The return to the embarkation beaches was harrowing. 43 RM Commando had recently been issued with lightweight felt-soled boots. These were excellent for silent movement at night, particularly on patrols, but they were inappropriate for fully loaded packs, and the sharp limestone rocks cut them to pieces. In C Troop a Marine wounded by mortar fire had to be carried all the way back. Four Marines fainted but were assisted. At 43 RM Commando's beach eight Marines were missing. Two days later Captain Bob Loudoun went back in an ML with a search party. Three Marines had managed to contact the Partisans, and these he rescued. The other five had become trapped in a minefield where one was killed and the others had been captured. When we joined the Commando at the beginning of August, the Marines in E Troop were still talking about their experiences on Mljet.

In their Seventh offensive at the end of May 1944 the Germans very nearly managed to eliminate Tito on his fifty-second birthday. He had established his HQ in a cave near the small settlement of Drvar so as to have the protection of solid rock above him. One day, a small plane, staying out of range, spent half an hour flying slowly up and down the valley, probably making a photographic reconnaissance. Three days later medium-sized aircraft circled round and bombed the village in turn. They were followed by six huge JU 52s, and soon the sky was full of billowing parachutes, with figures dangling beneath them. Then gliders came in, bringing more troops and guns. One glider made its approach immediately opposite the cave, but nose-dived and crashed, killing the troops on board. Nevertheless the Germans had established a heavy machine gun which commanded the steep path down from the cave – a Partisan who ventured forth was killed instantly. Fortunately the waterfall at the back of the cave was dry, and with the help of a rope the whole party managed to scramble up to the high ground above. Tito's huge Alsatian hound, Tiger, was hauled up as well. From the top of the cliff they were able to join up with Partisan units.

The Germans had committed strong forces to hunt down the Partisans and, like the rest, Tito was constantly on the move at night, and had to lie up in the woods by day. This made it impossible for him to coordinate the activities of all his forces, so he sent an urgent request to both Allied Forces HQ and to the Partisan commanders on Vis for an attack to be mounted in Dalmatia to try to relieve the pressure. The RAF gave immediate support by bombing and shooting up German concentrations in Bosnia. A British/Partisan planning group was hurriedly convened, and although their attitudes towards military tactics differed considerably, they decided to mount a large-scale combined operation on Brac.

The island was defended by 1200 men from the 118 Gebirgsjaeger Mountain Division, supported by artillery units. One garrison was in the northern port of Supetar; there was another in the eastern port of Sumartin; and their

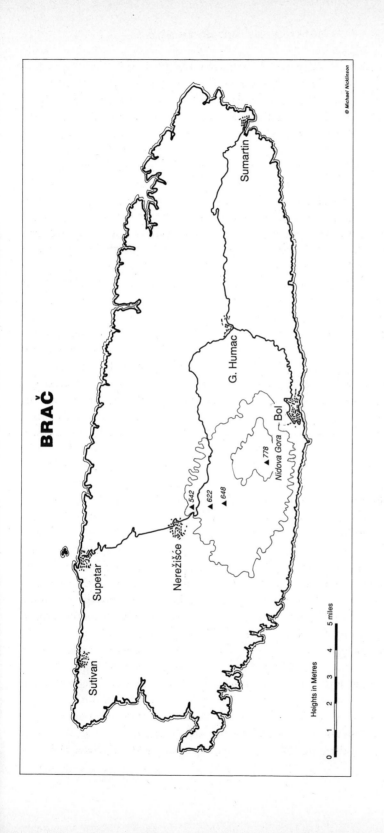

BRAČ

Sutivan

Supetar

Nerežišće

▲ 542

▲ 622

▲ 648

G. Humac

▲ 778

Nidova Gora

Bol

Sumartin

Heights in Metres

0   1   2   3   4   5 miles

© Michael Nicklinson

strongest position was in the centre of the island south-east of Nerezisce. Three hilltop fortifications – 542 (metres high), 622 and 648 – had mutual fire-support, which proved to be most effective. Communication difficulties led to failure of mutual support among the British/Yugoslav forces. The Partisans did not always fulfil their commitments, and there was crucial lack of wireless contact between the Commandos.

During the night of 1 June 1944 forty-five ships – 'Jug' schooners and naval craft – took 2500 Partisans and 43 RM Commando (augmented by 40 RM Commando's Heavy Weapons Troop) across to landing beaches on the south coast of Brac on Operation 'Flounced'. LCTs brought a battery of 25-pounders from 111 Field Regiment and a Troop of mountain guns from Raiding Support Regiment. Lieutenant Colonel Jack Churchill was the overall British Force Commander. Two strong Partisan groups headed across to Supetar and Sumartin respectively. They were unable to capture the towns, but did prevent reinforcements from being sent to the central position.

By dawn on 2 June 43 RM Commando was in position to attack 542, and Prekamorska battalions were ready to assault the other two hill features. Hurricanes flew in shortly after dawn to soften up the defences but, significantly, they did not cause much material damage to the log-roofed pill-boxes. By the time the Commandos and the Partisans reached the wire and minefields the Germans had resumed their fire positions. None of the attacks was able to penetrate the defences, and they were called off. It was decided to mount a combined attack on 542 in the afternoon, 43 RM Commando coming in from the north, and the Partisans from the south. The eight 25-pounders of Major Pat Turner's battery put down an effective half-hour barrage which covered the advance of the Commandos up the hill, but while it was in progress a woman interpreter reached 43 HQ with the message that the Partisans would not be taking part. Lieutenant Colonel Simonds decided to carry on. The Gunners' shoot was accurate, but the shells were not powerful enough to penetrate the strongly constructed bunkers. Bangalore torpedoes were pushed through the wire and detonated, but Spandaus soon concentrated on the gaps, and casualties mounted. Mortar fire from the other two hilltop positions intensified, and at 1645 hrs German troops were observed to be moving towards 542 for a counter-attack. Without Partisan support the flank of the three assault Troops was exposed, so Lieutenant Colonel Simonds requested further artillery fire to cover a withdrawal. 43 RM Commando went into all-round defence for the night of 2–3 June.

Reports began to reach Vis that the Germans were preparing to send more troops to Brac, so the three reserve Troops of 40 RM Commando under Lieutenant Colonel 'Pops' Manners embarked on a LCI and landed to re-inforce the British contingent at 0345 hours on 3 June. Some 300 more Partisans went over, too, and two more 25-pounder guns. Colonel Jack sent orders to 43 RM Commando to mount a night attack on 622 commencing at 2030 hrs, but unfortunately Lieutenant Colonel Simonds was unaware that the three Troops of 40 RM Commando were available to assist. The Partisans had agreed to 'harass' 542 and 648 while the attack was in progress. 111 Field bombarded the German position and 43 RM Commando set off on time, but the outcome was the same as in daylight. C Troop on the left still had a Bangalore torpedo to breach a gap, but the first two men to charge through were both hit. D Troop in the centre suffered casualties from small-arms, Spandaus, rifle-grenades and mortars, and were pinned down. B Troop on the right reached some outlying German trenches, but could get no further. All the officers in the assault group except one were killed or wounded, and four of the sergeants were casualties. Mortar fire from the other two German positions intensified to cover a counter-attack, and by this time ammunition among the Commandos was running out. At 2230 hours Lieutenant Colonel Simonds ordered a withdrawal. B Troop either did not receive the message or else they could not implement it, as they remained on the hill. Colonel Jack could not be contacted by wireless.

Colonel Jack carried out a daylight recce of 622 before he drew up his detailed orders, and it took him five hours to cover the ground. When he got back to his HQ his plan was for 40 RM Commando to attack from a different direction at the same time as 43. He was unable to make wireless contact with 40 RM Commando, so he dispatched the orders with a Staff officer. A Partisan who accompanied him was supposed to know the way but they both got hopelessly lost. Time was slipping by, so Colonel Jack set off himself and made contact with Lieutenant Colonel Manners, who was on his way to find him. Because of these delays it was not until 2130 hrs that the three Troops (A, Y, and Q) were organised on their start-line. After brief orders they commenced their advance, not knowing whether 43 RM Commando had taken the position or not. On their way up they came across B Troop of 43, so knew that they would be opposed. Bayonets were fixed, and there was close-quarter fighting to take outlying German trenches. Six German prisoners were taken, but enemy fire was heavy. Five officers were killed during the assault. A small band, including both Colonels, reached the summit, but found that the main body of the enemy had withdrawn. The reason soon became clear. Heavy mortar fire from 542 and 648 preceded a German counter-attack. In a last attempt to contact the rest of 43 RM Commando, Colonel Jack rolled over on his back and played 'Will ye no' come back again' on his pipes. Shortly afterwards the counter-attack came in. In the flurry of grenades a fragment cut a furrow in his helmet and knocked him unconscious. When he came to, German soldiers were standing over him and he was taken prisoner. The much-respected 'Pops' Manners had twice been badly hit, and sadly he died from his wounds. Major Maude extricated the three Troops of 40 RM Commando back to the start line, together with the remnants of B Troop 43 RM Commando, whose Commander, Captain Schooley, had been killed.

When Colonel Jack was reported missing, Lieutenant Colonel Simonds took over as Force Commander and organised the withdrawal of all troops back to Vis on 4 June. Two ME 109s tried to strafe the beaches, but Spitfires appeared and shot them down. Both 2 Commando and 40 RM Commando sent over search parties to try to trace those who had failed to return. Strong German patrols were sweeping the island, and some of the 2 Commando party were captured. Little news was gathered before both groups returned empty-handed.

The 'diversion' was costly to the Commandos. They lost two highly talented leaders, with long experience. 43 RM Commando had two officers killed, four officers wounded, thirteen Other Ranks killed or missing, and forty-seven wounded. 40 RM Commando had nineteen killed or captured, and forty wounded. Partisan casualties numbered 260. Intelligence assessment was that 1900 Germans were sent to Brac to sweep the island. No troops were diverted from Bosnia, but on the other hand no reinforcements were sent from Dalmatia to assist the Seventh offensive.

Tito decided that he and the British and Russian Missions would have to be evacuated from the mainland. On 3–4 June 1944 a Dakota managed to pick out the bonfires lit on flat land at Kupreska Polje, and landed by moonlight. Tito, half a dozen members of his staff, his faithful dog Tiger, General Korneynev and his Russian Mission, and Colonel Vivian Street, Rifle Brigade, climbed aboard. The plane was manned by a Russian crew, as the Dakota had been given to the Soviet Union under lend-lease, and was flying out of Bari under British operational control.

Vis was the one place in Yugoslavia where Tito could resume undisturbed command, and on 13 June 1944 the crew of the destroyer HMS *Blackmore* entertained him convivially during his passage across to the island. He must have had a penchant for caves, as again he chose one on Mount Hum for his HQ. At a ceremonial parade to greet his arrival, the Marshal inspected 2 Commando. His address included the following extracts:

> On this occasion I want to express my gratitude to you and the gratitude of our people for the sacrifices and efforts you have given, far away from your home, here, on the soil of Yugoslavia, for our common goal, the liberation of the People of Europe from the detested Fascist occupier. The gallantry and self-sacrifice of No. 2 Commando in the battles on the islands of Brac, Korcula, Solta and others is well known and much valued. …
>
> I am happy to have been convinced personally that here, on this island, a perfect concord and comradeship in arms exists between you and our Army of National Liberation. This island symbolises that friendship and comradeship in war which unites all the Allies.

*   *   *

In August 1944 a number of small parties went on recces, and ambushes were planned and prepared for, but we 'new boys' began to get a little disillusioned when none of them came off. I put in for a parachute course, but eight officers of 2 Commando had been away on it in Italy when the Brac operation suddenly came up, so it was no longer sanctioned. Perhaps as compensation I was sent on a short course on Combined Operations. It was still dark as we approached Bari and farther north up the coast there were diffused flashes in the sky which continued for some time. I thought that at last I was getting nearer some action, but was puzzled that it was going on so far south. Not until some time later did it dawn on me that it must have been a thunderstorm. The course was held near Benevento, and we were fully briefed on all the planning for the Sicily, Salerno and Anzio landings, but what I remember most was an evening get-together. A Maori officer got going after some drink, and his high melodic singing of Maori songs was hauntingly emotional. Unwisely I mixed my drinks, and when I lay back on my bed there was the ghastly feeling of the room beginning to revolve. I just made it to the loo to be violently sick, which eased the situation. Switching to vermouth did the damage, and I have not touched it since.

I returned to Vis on the morning of 11 September 1944, and PC told me to get my marching order ready straight away, as the Commando was off on an operation. Within an hour I was on my way back to the harbour. Having just learnt about the detailed loading of all the landing craft for the three seaborne assaults it was amusing to watch gear being slung on to the LCI as it arrived, to be stowed anywhere that there was space. It turned out that we were off to Brac again at short notice, as Partisan intelligence had reported that the Germans had pulled back from all outlying positions. This time two Partisan 'Brigades' (much smaller than ours) were detailed to capture the Germans before they left the island, and our job was to protect their flank to the north-west, and to give help if necessary.

We were landed on the south coast at night, and had a tiring heavy-laden ten-mile march up and down over the mountains in hot sunshine the next day. At one stage I was slogging uphill with half the Troop when a couple of Spitfires came into view, and we all waved cheerily towards them. One wheeled towards us, and we were expecting him to wave back. All of a sudden we realised from the angle of his dive that his intentions were hostile. There was a small ditch beside the road and we flattened ourselves along it seconds before the bursts of machine-gun fire cracked into the hillside and the plane zoomed up just above us. My fourth close encounter with 'friendly' fire. No one was hit, and we released our feelings of shock and furious indignation by swearing profusely. The men were particularly incensed as the same thing had happened on the previous Brac operation, and they told me that two Marines had been wounded. HQ Balkan Air Force had failed to inform its pilots of our presence on the island.

Eventually we reached Sutivan, a small fishing village on the north coast, where there were some Partisans about, but not many civilians. I was taken along the quay to be proudly shown a drowned Italian armoured vehicle with a small gun turret which had been pushed over during the occupation. As I was conveying suitable admiration, a fisherman landed an octopus near the spot. A Partisan slapped it on a bollard, bashed away at its head, then cut off a tentacle and offered it to me. When I politely declined he began to chew it himself. Many of the small cottages were deserted and looked as if they had recently been occupied by troops, as their contents were strewn all over the floors. Always inquisitive, I spent some time sifting through the debris, and to my complete astonishment, in this unlikely place, I came across an English translation of Virgil's *Aeneid* Book VI. This had been my set book for School Certificate, and mastering an English crib had helped me to get through.

After PC's recce we took up our positions on a ridge inland of Sutivan where we looked across at Supetar, three miles to the east, the objective for one of the Partisan brigades. Next day we learned that they had been just too late, as the garrison had escaped to Split during the night. The Navy managed to block-ade the other small port, Sumartin, in the extreme south-east of the island. The garrison resisted the attacks of the combined Partisan forces, supported by the guns of 111 Field and the RSR (Raiding Support Regiment), for over a week, but this time BAF (Balkan Air Force) medium-bombers and fighter-bombers came in, and the combined operations led to the capture of about 200 prisoners. We were not involved, and the Commando returned to Vis on 15 September.

Two days later we were back again, this time to Solta island which lies only half a mile west of Brac, close to the mainland. Recent aerial reconnaissance had indicated that the garrison was about to withdraw. We landed at night, and there was a steep scramble up, but instead of the freedom to climb, as in Cornwall, we were very heavily laden. Since 111 Field were not with us, there was only the Heavy Weapons Troop to provide supporting fire. Each of us had to carry either two 3-inch mortar bombs (10 pounds each) or belts of Vickers ammunition in his large pack, in addition to full Bren magazines (Tommy-gun magazines in my case), Mills and smoke grenades, and the weapons themselves. Live ammunition weighs much more than training blanks. Not only were the hillsides steep, there were retaining walls to provide terraces for vines, and sur-mounting these was particularly exhausting. I have never been so glad as when I reached the stock-pile position and dumped those damn bombs.

D and E Troops were given the task of taking two fortified outposts on the highest points on the island, Vela Straza and Mala Straza. As we were advanc-ing in open formation down a forward slope towards them, they opened up on us with machine-gun and mortar fire, fortunately at long range. There was completely inadequate cover, so Ian and PC wisely decided to lie up, and to approach in the dark. PC had a rugby badge of the 'Red Hand of Ulster' on a white background which he pinned to his back to be visible for us to follow. That night, as we came close to the objective, I had the sickening shock of stumbling over a trip-wire, but there was no explosion. Although it meant temporary bunching, I held the wire in two hands as a step-over point for the section, and we silently did the same for succeeding wires as I cautiously felt my way forward. There were no bursts of fire from the enemy. Eventually we got right through to the defensive position, and found to our relief that it had been recently evacuated, or almost so. They left behind a fierce German wolfhound guard-dog, which fulfilled its role all too well. Nothing we could do would drive it away, and its bared fangs made it dangerous for us to move freely. In the end there was no option but to shoot it, a task that I absolutely hated. When dawn broke we were able to see the formidable array of stick-mines through which we had come. I crawled out and examined one of them, to discover that I had got away with it because the normally efficient Germans had left the string safety ties on the detonators!

For the next couple of days life became distinctly unpleasant. We set up defensive positions away from the objective, as we knew that the heavy mainland batteries at Split and Trogir had the accurate range. This involved building protective stone sangars, as digging-in was impossible in the hard limestone. I found an old mattress in one of the dugouts, and was highly pleased with this soft base for my sangar until I later made the unwelcome discovery that the Germans had secret allies. Lice and fleas transferred themselves, and congregated around my waist. Sure enough, the shelling started. After hearing the boom we timed the flight before the whistle and crash came in – about fifty seconds. The snag was that the 81mm mortars in the main German positions north-east of Grohote also had the range, and their high-trajectory bombs crumped in without warning while we awaited a shell – disconcerting. There is a curious excitement from long-range shelling – the die is cast, and one has time to ponder on the lottery of impact. Mortars have nothing going for them: they shake one up with their sudden surprise. Our own 3-inch mortars and Vickers machine-guns were now able to fire on the main position, but this made the Germans retaliate more. There were surprisingly few casualties from all this bombardment, though we heard shrapnel crack into the rocks of our sangars. When I went across to D Troop I found that Ian Gourlay had a scalp wound that was not serious, but he looked impressive with a field dressing swathed around his head, and his tin hat perched high.

For the initial approach march there had been the usual hot sunshine. The next day the weather changed dramatically. In early autumn depressions begin to penetrate into the Adriatic, and if they are deep they draw down colder bora winds from the Dinaric plateau. This one was deep. The chilling winds blew with increasing force, accompanied by sheets of rain, against which it was

impossible to avoid getting soaked. The combination of shelling and bad
weather meant that no replenishment supplies reached us for two days, so we
went hungry, and had to catch water in ground sheets. Eventually the
Adjutant, George Frost, made a hazardous journey along the coast in a small
LCP to get 24-hour packs and ammunition within reach. I have come across a
message which my erudite signaller wrote in pencil on the margin of my map
as he received it:

To Sunray Minor.
   Dog and Easy send carrying parties to BE8521, LCP will bring your supplies.
Signals by torch. Recognition letter S for Sugar to LCP. ETA (estimated time of
arrival) follows. Make shure BE9032 and 8035 are denide to enemy.

The enemy did not interfere, and George Frost was a very popular man.
   Our CO, Lieutenant Colonel Ian MacAlpine, had requested artillery and air
support, but rough seas and poor visibility made it impossible for this to reach
us from Vis. Neither could the Germans escape by sea. Despite the weather we
patrolled northward, and found that the three villages in the polje, Donje Selo,
Srednje Selo and Grohote, were deserted, but when we probed farther east we
drew enemy fire, which enabled us to locate several strongpoints. After dusk on
the second day E Troop moved north through Grohote and took up a position
closest to the enemy on the forward slope of the ridge rising west of Rogac harbour. By then the rain had stopped, the wind had died down, and there was a
starlit sky. Preliminary orders had been given for a dawn attack, and thinking
about the strength of the fortifications facing us was not conducive to sleep.
In the still air we could hear the muted commands and movements of the
Germans.
   In the middle of the night, to my intense surprise, a calm order in English
came up as clear as a bell – 'I'm going in now. Prepare to give me covering fire.'
Shortly afterwards pandemonium broke loose. The clatter of Oerlikons shattered the stillness; tracer rounds sped across the darkness below, and ricocheted
up into the sky; there was a loud explosion; cries and screams of anguish broke
out, and there were sounds of utter confusion. When the firing eventually
ceased, the sudden silence came as a sharp contrast. The voice, still as professional, unemotional and steady, came up clearly for the second time – 'I reckon
we've got them. Ease your way out slow astern, and I'll follow you.' In the
darkness we could see nothing, though we had a good idea of what had
happened.
   Shortly after dawn we received the order to take Rogac. We spread out into
extended line, and began to move down. Suddenly there was an explosion on
the left flank, followed by two more near the centre. Three Marines sustained
serious leg injuries. The slope had been sown with schu-mines. These are

thoroughly pernicious – a small wooden box about 6 in × 4 in contains a charge beneath a compressional lid resting on the projections from a bakelite detonator. PC ordered everyone to stand still. Then he told the Marines on either side of the wounded men to move in carefully and give assistance. They did what they could for them, then one took all the equipment while the other hoisted his unfortunate comrade in a fireman's lift. It would have taken hours to prod our way out, and the wounded men would have suffered more, so PC and I mutually agreed to chance it down. All the Marines were told to tread exactly in the footsteps of the man in front, and to form two single files behind us. The rocky slope was covered in maquis – small bushes of lavender, thyme and rosemary: ideal for concealing those mines. Cautiously I advanced one step at a time, feeling apprehension during the forward movement, then tension as my weight came down. During the spells of action one lived to a unique intensity. Luck held for both of us, and after what seemed an age we reached a road, which was safe, and got a message to Doc Bazeley that three stretchers were needed.

A Troop had been similarly trapped on the slope east of the harbour. One of their men was killed, and five had their feet blown off. They had a Sapper attached, Lieutenant Richards, who spent hours prodding and lifting schu-mines to get people out, so it was tragic that in the end he too lost a foot. He was awarded the Military Cross, as were Ian Gourlay and PC for their fine leadership.

As we advanced tactically down the road there were occasional clusters of red objects on shrubs on the banks. I thought they might be small red Italian hand-grenades, but couldn't work out how they would act as booby-traps. There was no time to investigate. Later in Italy I came across ripe pomegranates in a shop – that is what they must have been. When we reached the strangely deserted harbour, five demoralised German soldiers immediately came forward and gave themselves up. The garrison had embarked on three lighters and as they were heading out towards the mouth of the bay they were attacked and sunk by two MTBs. Well over a hundred unfortunate men must have been drowned. We were mighty relieved that, by the slimmest of margins, we did not have to fight them. With such inadequate fire support we would undoubtedly have had heavy losses. The island was freed from German occupation for the last time.

I walked out to the end of the jetty with Tipton and Pillinger, and there were bodies bobbing far out. One had drifted farther in, so we hunted round, found a small rowing boat, and brought the German ashore for identification. I had my eye on a pistol at his waist, which turned out to be a P38. Pillinger said he knew something about them, so I handed it to him. The clearing mechanism was stiff, and I thought that after immersion it probably would not work. Pillinger continued to struggle with it, and knelt down to get a better purchase on his knee. Suddenly it gave, and as it clicked back a shot rang out. In the stunned silence I found myself looking down at a groove chipped out of the concrete between my heels. My fifth very close encounter with 'friendly' fire.

The colour came back to Pillinger's face, and he looked completely abashed. We all fully realised how foolish we had been, and no more was said. Nevertheless I did clean and oil the pistol and brought it back to England; but my mother wisely persuaded me to hand it in when there was an amnesty on unlicenced weapons.

Back on Vis, E Troop was selected for an ambush on Sveti Arhandel off Split, to waylay E-boats which sometimes put in. Planning and rehearsals were detailed, but in the end it was cancelled.

On 17 October 1944 the Commando left Vis for the last time, and landed in Italy. I remember that I was desperately tired when we arrived, and had the greatest difficulty keeping awake to map-read my convoy to Putignano. Here the officers were allocated 'civvy billets', and the men occupied a barracks – our first reintroduction to buildings for a long time. I had a small bedroom on my own in a tall apartment house which had an outdoor iron staircase spiralling up from a small inner courtyard. The family below were intrigued and friendly, but we did not get much further than an exchange of 'Buon giorno', and 'Molta grazia' for small favours. They had a daughter of about sixteen who had a good voice and was always singing operatic arias, but it was her fully developed firm figure that made me long to try to entice her into bed. I was too gauche to pluck up the courage to make a move, though my feeling that she was a completely innocent young girl may have influenced me. The South Africans were much more worldly wise, and took full advantage of their stay. PC had a Troop photograph taken in Putignano. There were fifty-five of us, whereas seventy should have been the official establishment.

Mediterranean countries are notorious for their poor plumbing. Gradually all the lavatories in the barracks became blocked, and when the Adjutant decided that the problem had to be tackled I was the hapless Duty Officer to whom he gave the plans of the drains. E Troop were on duty, and I set the lucky half of the fatigue party to digging a pit. The remainder came with me, and we lifted the first drain cover and surveyed the filthy mess. The space was too restricted to use a shovel, and the Marines shifted uneasily from foot to foot. Rather than give unpleasant orders, I decided that leadership was called for, so I stripped off to my pants, plunged my hands in, and started scooping out into a bucket. When I had done my stint the next man made no complaint at doing the same thing, and as we carried on in rotation at each access point we began to take a grim satisfaction in exposing the pipes and clearing them as far as we could reach, as we had no rods. Finally we tackled the loos, which were the hole-in-the-floor squatting type. Then came the acid test. After continued flushing they at last cleared. Filthy and smelly, we grinned at each other, and went off for well-earned scrub-downs. Most of the Commando were unaware, except perhaps by smell, of the unsung heroes who had improved their lot. Two days later we moved, and another unit reaped the benefit. Such are the joys of life behind the lines.

CHAPTER 4

Internal Feuds in Yugoslavia

This part of the Balkans lies athwart the cultural crossroads between Europe and Asia – Roman, Byzantine, Slav, Teuton and Ottoman Turk. It was in Sarajevo that Archduke Franz Ferdinand was assassinated by a young Bosnian Serb student, which sparked off the First World War. Serbia fought on the Allied side, and suffered severely at the hands of the Austro-German and Bulgarian armies. Established in 1918 to meet the aspirations of the separated South Slavs, Yugoslavia was an amalgamation of seven distinctive regions which had marked differences in ethnic origin, political history, language and religion. There were even two scripts: Latin in the west of the country and Cyrillic in the east. The more sophisticated Slovenes and Croats were Catholic; the Bosnians mainly Moslem: all had been under different administrations within the Austro-Hungarian Empire. The Eastern Orthodox Serbs and the Montenegrins had a long history of resistance to Turkish rule. Serbia gained independence in 1878, but Montenegro not until 1912.

The Serbs were the largest group, and with their history of independence and their King as the new head of state they expected to dominate a unified Yugoslavia governed from Belgrade. The Croats had other ideas. They wanted semi-autonomy within a federal framework, but there were considerable enclaves of Serbian settlement within Croatian territory. Their leader Radic was imprisoned during the first (and only) free election in 1920, so the Croats refused to sit in the Constituent Assembly. This played into the hands of the Serbs, who were able to get a majority to pass a centralised constitution in 1921. Fifty-eight Communist deputies were elected to the legislature, but in 1922 a Communist assassinated the Minister of the Interior, so the Party was banned. Then in 1928 a Montenegrin deputy shot dead Radic and two other Croats in the Assembly building. King Alexander suspended the constitution until 1931, and gave the security police, the great majority of whom were Serbs, a free hand in curbing opposition. In October 1934 Alexander went on a state visit to France away from his close protection at home, and a Croat Ustasa extremist assassinated him in Marseilles. His son Peter was only eleven, so the King's cousin Paul was appointed Regent.

Mihailovic served with distinction in the Serbian army in the First World War. After the capitulation in 1941 he avoided capture, and began to organise Serbian soldiers into a resistance movement. They were known as Cetniks after the former guerrillas who fought the Turks. Everyone remained bearded, and the Royal Arms were worn in their tall sheepskin caps. Mihailovic had the initial advantage that his men were better trained and armed than the Partisans, but his policy of husbanding his resources led to long periods of inactivity which sapped the morale of his men, and he found it increasingly difficult to control the activities of his subordinates.

There was another split in Serbia. As with Pétain in Vichy France, Hitler put the compliant General Nedic in charge of a puppet government, which worked in cooperation with the Germans.

Josip Broz, the son of a Croat peasant, was conscripted into the Austro-Hungarian army in 1913. He acquitted himself well as an NCO, at first fighting the Serbs, and then the Russians, where he was wounded and taken prisoner by the Tsarist forces. When the Bolshevik Revolution occurred, prisoners of war were set free. Broz was attracted to the Communist ideology, and served in the Red Army throughout the civil war. When he returned to Yugoslavia the Party had been banned, but he was a dedicated revolutionary and for the next twenty years he was in and out of prison, in hiding, or in exile. He recruited some 1500 volunteers in Yugoslavia to serve in the International Brigades, and helped them to reach Spain. In 1937 the Communist International appointed him as Secretary-General of the Yugoslav Communist Party, and he became an excellent underground organiser. The story is told that so often did he say 'Do this, do that' – 'Ti' 'to' in Serbo-Croat – that it became his nickname.

Ante Pavelic had gone into exile in Italy after his terrorist activities. A French court had condemned him to death in his absence for his connection with the murder of Alexander. After becoming dictator of Croatia, he rivalled Hitler in his atrocities. As a fanatical Croat nationalist his aim was to kill or force to flee all the one and a half million Serbs who had settled over the centuries in Croatia. As a Fascist he extended his purges to Jews and Gypsies. All this as a devout Catholic! Estimates of the slaughter of innocent men, women and children which took place throughout the summer of 1941 exceed 600,000, and the Orthodox churches were destroyed. Bitter necessity provided many recruits for the resistance movements.

When the Cetniks and Partisans began their initially successful guerrilla activities the Germans were equally ruthless in their reprisals. In October 1941 the Partisans ambushed a German column on its way back to Kragujevac in Serbia, killing twelve soldiers and wounding twenty-six. The German response was indiscriminately to round up men and boys from the town, march them off in batches, and machine-gun them down. The estimates are that over 3000 were executed. Six hundred were kept as hostages to prevent further attacks, and several hundred eye-witnesses were released so that word would be spread. The savagery was unimaginable. It is probable that Yugoslavia suffered heavier losses proportionally than any other European country. One estimate is that one and three quarter million people lost their lives – an eighth of the pre-war population: not to mention all the houses destroyed and children left orphaned.

After the Teheran Conference in December 1943 Churchill strongly urged King Peter to dissociate himself from Mihailovic, but Peter did not do so until May 1944.

Tito, thanks to Fitzroy Maclean's high-level contacts, achieved political recognition on the Western world scene on 12 August 1944, when he discussed the future of Yugoslavia personally with Churchill in Naples. General Wilson promised to do his best to meet Tito's requests for the war material he needed, and supplies steadily increased through the British Mission's liaison with Allied HQ at Caserta. Then, in late September, Tito mysteriously disappeared from Vis without a word to anyone, causing an interruption in the coordination. When Churchill went to Moscow on 9 October 1944 he discovered that Tito had been there beforehand. Later, when he renewed contact with Tito in Serbia, Maclean found out that the Yugoslav leader had boldly made it clear to Stalin that he must remain in control of the country. He had proposed that the battle for Belgrade should be a joint operation between his Partisans and the Red Army. Stalin had been willing to do this, and further agreed that Russian forces would leave Yugoslavia afterwards.

Churchill was understandably annoyed at what he called this 'secret levanting' and 'graceless behaviour', but he reached agreement with Stalin that the influence of Britain and the Soviet Union over a post-war settlement in Yugoslavia should be fifty-fifty. In his fine literary style he expressed the position as follows:

> There should be joint action and an agreed policy between the two Powers now closely involved, so as to favour the creation of a united Yugoslavia after all elements there have been joined together to the utmost in driving out the Nazi invaders. It is intended to prevent, for instance, armed strife between the Croats and Slovenes on the one side and powerful and numerous elements in Serbia on the other, and also to produce a joint and friendly policy towards Marshal Tito while ensuring that weapons furnished to him are used against the common Nazi foe rather than for internal purposes.

At the beginning of September 1944 Romania and Bulgaria had both capitulated and had been occupied by Russian forces. On the Western Front there was a link-up on 11 September 1944 at Sombernon, just west of Dijon, between Eisenhower's army and US/Free French forces who had advanced up the Rhône–Saône valley after landing on the south coast of France. Russian tanks, artillery and aircraft played a key role in overcoming German resistance in Belgrade, which was finally taken on 21 October 1944. General von Lohr

Above: LCI with 43 RM Commando on board approaching Gruz harbour, 13 October 1944.

Right: Disembarking at Dubrovnik. The Partisan photographer is about to raise his forage cap in a polite English manner.

Bill Jenkins signalling that he was no picture postcard.

ʈove: 5 November ceremonial parade in Dubrovnik, 44. Major Harding, A Troop (saluting), was in ɱmand. Captain Ian Gourlay, D Troop, is centre left.

Marine Fred Beale is on the extreme left, front row.
Below: The main road, not far from Niksic.

Above: Montenegrin village.
Left: Mike McConville wearing a leather jerkin in Montenegro. Life on the upland plateau was harsh in winter.
Opposite page, top: Partisans loading a stripped-down 75mm American Pack Howitzer, known colloquially as a 'mountain-gun'. They were trained by British personnel at the Balkan School of Artillery on Vis. (IWM NA.18291)
Opposite page, bottom: The breech-block fitted above the wheels. (IWM NA.18292)

Opposite page, top: The Pack Howitzer split into five mule loads. The barrel was the really awkward load. (IWM NA.18293)

Opposite page, bottom: Sgt. W. Lewis of the Balkan School teaching male and female Partisans how to operate a long-range wireless set. (IWM NA.18294)

Above: General Radovan Vukanovic, commanding Partisan II Corps, at a liaison meeting with Brigadier J. P. O'Brien-Twohig, commander Floydforce, Niksic, 23 November 1944. (IWM NA.20333)

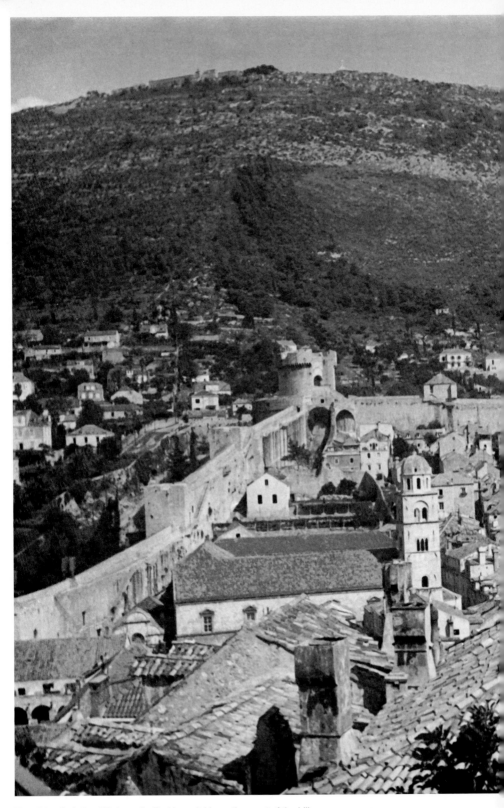

The old walled city of Dubrovnik; Fort Imperial is on the crest of the hill.

was forced to organise the full withdrawal of his Army Group 'E' from Greece, Albania and southern Yugoslavia.

With the fall of Belgrade, Tito had *de facto* political control in the capital. Communist cadres were firmly established in all the regions, though they remained a minority. At the end of November 1944 Tito set up a Provisional Government, proclaiming that it had the sole authority to represent the Yugoslav nation. Britain still recognised King Peter and his government-in-exile, but Churchill was prepared to leave this difficult problem until Yugoslavia had been liberated. When this had been achieved, Tito pressed the point that it was he and his Partisans who had won freedom for Yugoslavia, and his adroit political manoeuvring led to the recognition of his government over the whole country. King Peter remained in exile; Mihailovic was tried and executed in 1946; Serbia and all the other provinces came under firm Communist control. In 1972 Queen Elizabeth II paid an official royal visit to President Tito.

CHAPTER 5

Floydforce in Montenegro

The move from Putignano was back to Yugoslavia, this time to Montenegro, where we learned at first hand about the hardships and bitter feuds. When we landed at Dubrovnik we were part of a command renamed Land Forces Adriatic. This must have aroused the suspicions of the Communist commissars as to whether the Allies were planning a strategic move into Yugoslavia. In point of fact General Alexander did put forward a proposal for a two-handed punch on Trieste for February 1945 – the Eighth Army across the Adriatic, and the Fifth up from Italy. The Combined Chiefs of Staff were planning a major winter offensive in northern Europe, and wanted German troops to be held down in Italy, so the plan was not authorised.

The attempt to impede the withdrawal of Army Group E was left mainly to the Balkan Air Force, and 'the use of light forces to operate with the Partisans'. The Russians had swung north into Hungary after the fall of Belgrade, giving the Germans a chance to regroup in Northern Yugoslavia. Vlatco Velebit, one of Tito's personal representatives, was in Bari in October 1944. A conference was hastily arranged between him and Air Vice-Marshal Elliot, Commander of the Balkan Air Force, and Brigadier Davy, Commander of Land Forces Adriatic. They offered a force of artillery and engineers, escorted by a Commando, to support the local Partisans in their attempt to cut off the retreat of XXI Gebirgsjaeger Korps. Six Hurricanes, protected by an RAF Regiment detachment, could be spared to operate from an airstrip in Montenegro. Velebit got in touch with Tito, who gave his approval. He needed the air and artillery support, but was unwilling for a body of British assault troops to take away any glory from the Partisans. Instead of the cheerful and friendly relations which we had enjoyed on Vis, the Commando bore the brunt of Communist distrust, and the Montenegrin Partisan HQ deliberately blocked our plans for offensive operations. The situation that confronted us on the mainland led to frustration and annoyance.

The Germans withdrew from Dubrovnik on 21 October 1944. A week later 'Floydforce' disembarked on to the quays of Gruz harbour, about one and a half miles north-west of the old walled town. 43 RM Commando came across in LCIs, and the guns and support vehicles of 111 Field Regiment, a Troop from 64 HAA (Heavy Anti-Aircraft) Regiment, and a RSR detachment were brought in LCTs. There was a marked absence of any civilians, but a pre-war photographer (in Partisan uniform) took personal snaps, and I later tracked down his shop in the town and obtained some prints of myself in fighting order, without the large pack. The hotels on the eastern side of the Lapad peninsula were empty and had suffered varying degrees of vandalisation prior to the German departure. Some of us slept on the floors of empty rooms, and most of the men were in a large shed in a timber yard, which at least had a good roof.

When 21st Mountain Corps reached Montenegro from Albania, they had three possible escape routes – along the coast; up through Danilovgrad and Niksic; or further inland through Kolasin and Visegrad to join up with the main body from Greece.

C Troop were dispatched south the very next day with a battery of eight 25-pounders to assist the Primorska group of Partisans. They were containing Germans who held strong positions in the small port of Risan and the village of Ledinice just to the north. In addition, five well-sited Imperial Austrian forts were occupied in which steel-lined weapon slits had been built into the nineteenth-century 6ft-thick stone walls. A motorised column got through the Partisans on the Kotor road, so on 3 November 1944 B Troop were ordered to take up defensive positions astride the Viluse–Risan road to provide a backstop in case the Germans put in a determined advance. They had a cold, wet, uncomfortable time on the mountainsides for over two weeks, and saw nothing of the enemy.

The Gunners, now joined by two 75mm howitzers from the RSR and the 3-inch mortars and MMGs of our Heavy Weapons Troop, put down a tremendous weight of fire, which much impressed the Partisans. From a rock shelf 1600 feet up they had commanding views down on Risan and much of the Gulf of Kotor. High-explosive shells had no effect on the old forts, so armour-piercing solid shot was tried, and this gradually reduced them. Bob Loudoun (C Troop commander) carried out a heavily laden ten-mile march round the mountains with a small party of Marines and a Partisan guide and reached a road culvert about two miles south of Risan which was in view of the guns. He detonated a large demolition charge which effectively prevented heavy transport from using the supply route up from Kotor, as shelling deterred repair parties. Further heavy shelling brought about the surrender of the garrison in Ledinice on 17 November. They had put up a brave resistance, as forty-nine had been killed, seventy wounded, and 197 prisoners were taken unhurt. During the night of 21 November the Germans withdrew from Risan, so Floydforce played a major role in getting them to abandon this escape route. Their job done, they rejoined us up on the plateau.

In contrast, D and E Troops had to get down to spit and polish, as on 5 November we provided a British detachment for a ceremonial parade in the medieval town to celebrate the twenty-seventh anniversary of the Russian Revolution. A Partisan General and officers from the British, American and

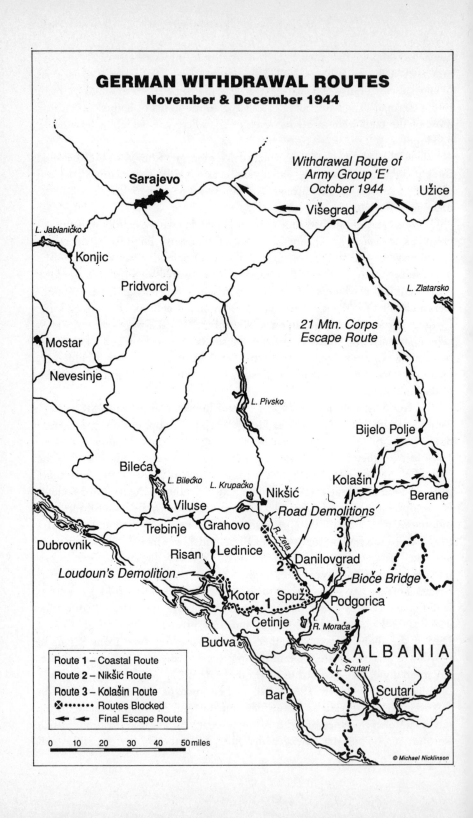

GERMAN WITHDRAWAL ROUTES
November & December 1944

Sarajevo

Withdrawal Route of Army Group 'E' October 1944

Užice

Višegrad

L. Jablaničko

Konjic

Pridvorci

L. Zlatarsko

21 Mtn. Corps Escape Route

Mostar

Nevesinje

L. Pivsko

Bijelo Polje

Bileća

L. Bilećko   *L. Krupačko*   Nikšić

Kolašin

Viluse

Road Demolitions

Berane

Trebinje   Grahovo

R. Zeta

3

Dubrovnik

Risan   Ledinice

2   Danilovgrad

Bioče Bridge

Loudoun's Demolition

Kotor   **1**   Spuž

Podgorica

Cetinje   *R. Morača*

Budva

A L B A N I A

L. Scutari

Bar

Scutari

Route **1** – Coastal Route
Route **2** – Nikšić Route
Route **3** – Kolašin Route
⊗ ••••• Routes Blocked
◀— ◀— Final Escape Route

0   10   20   30   40   50 miles

© *Michael Nicklinson*

Russian Missions addressed us in what were no doubt weighty words – they were delivered in Serbo-Croat. When darkness fell, bonfires lit up a huge ZIVIO TITO on the mountainside behind Dubrovnik. During the first few days it was interesting to visit the heavy gun emplacements defending Gruz so soon after the Germans had left. Panoramas on the walls above the gun-slits showed ranges to all the targets at a glance.

Drill over, we were deployed inland to defend against a possible thrust up the Niksic route. Approaching the town, we were winding slowly round a bend when we noticed two figures digging, stripped to the waist, behind a barrack-type building, watched by a group in greatcoats. The road took a long sweep round, and I was pondering on the hardiness of the diggers, when we came in sight again a bit closer. The two men finished digging and stood up; two great-coated figures stepped forward and raised their right arms towards their heads; there were convulsive jerks, and the half-naked bodies fell to the ground. We realised with revulsion that we had witnessed an execution. The Marines were very incensed, but there was nothing that we could do about it. The families with Cetnik husbands hiding in the hills would have to try to open the graves unobserved to find out who had been caught. On a later occasion I happened to be in a farmhouse when four Partisans came in and roughly questioned the housewife. The Serbo-Croat was unintelligible, but the terror in her eyes was not. She remained rooted to a chair while they carried out a very thorough search. Thankfully they did not find what they were looking for, so I did not have to get involved. I was amazed to discover how political divisions went right to the heart of peasant communities.

There was a dramatic change in our living conditions when we moved up on to the high barren plateau. Gone were the sunny terraced vineyards and cheerful songs of Dalmatia, with its Catholic churches and Venetian cultural heritage. Instead we met gaunt shepherds dressed in hairy cowskin cloaks, who lived at bare subsistence level. The songs were eastern dirges. At an outdoor village dance in which, instead of the lively Dalmatian flings, they just circled one way and then the other, I heard a curious noise. On turning round I dis-covered that it was a local custom to spit over the shoulder. The churches were mainly Greek Orthodox, with a few mosques from the period of Turkish domination. In winter, at an altitude of just under 3000 feet, the nights were bitter, but the Montenegrins were so poor that we often had to bivouac. No tents were available, as our transport was limited, and we were frequently on the move. On one memorable occasion, when we were in a roofless outhouse, it rained almost continuously for seven days and nights. Time and again the groundsheets we rigged could not hold the water despite judicious upward pressure for tipping, and they collapsed. Wet through, and chilled to the bone at night, it needed a tremendous effort of will to warm up compo on Tommy cookers. Wood was scarce, and we could hardly deprive the peasants by excessive scavenging. I suppose it says something that none of us went down from exposure, as we had very little spare clothing; the kitbags with our great-coats and change of clothing never caught up with us, so we only had sleeveless leather jerkins. Thus we had only the battledress that we stood up in, which was worn day and night. The CO managed to obtain authorisation for an issue of Navy rum after the rain ordeal. One tot does not last long, but it went down well. Snow came in December, and visits to the alfresco latrines were another test of endurance. If we had been doing a useful job we would not have minded these harsh conditions, but most of the time we were living rough to no great purpose. Our friendly exchanges with local Partisan commanders would often be interrupted by the appearance of a saturnine, unsmiling political commissar, who brought the attempts at fraternisation to a close. I was with one of these men, who spoke a little English, when a Hurricane flew over, so I told him its name. He would have none of it: nothing I could say shifted him from his belief that the plane had been Russian. The hard-core Communists stuck rigidly to the party line.

If pressure developed, the plan was to blow the bridge at Niksic, so 579 Field Company of the Royal Engineers fixed demolition charges on all fifteen of the stone-built piers that supported it. Our job was to set up defensive positions to cover the bridge, and to man forward positions on the mountainsides at the head of the Zeta valley, from which patrols moved south. A spell of duty here was physically demanding and militarily unrewarding, as the Germans only advanced as far as Danilovgrad to protect the flank of their main exodus inland towards Kolasin. When the Partisan Commander introduced a new feature – reports of German movements south from Mostar and Nevesinje – E Troop was moved to Bileca to defend the road from the north. I still have the 1/100,000 maps which we used. The Dubrovnik and Trebinje sheets were printed in Roman script, but those for Niksic and Cetinje were copied from 1928 maps in Cyrillic, with just the names of towns overprinted in red.

Mostar is in Herzegovina, and I began to think about the Ustase. After all the horror stories of the tortures that they carried out, I was really concerned not to fall into their hands. Stuck out in Bileca we were about fifty miles away by road from the rest of the Commando. One day a jeep pulled up outside our billet bristling with a .50 calibre Browning machine gun pintle-mounted in front of the passenger seat alongside the driver and a Bren mounted on a tripod at the rear. It was an LRDG (Long Range Desert Group) patrol which had been much more isolated than ourselves. The officer stepped out, shook hands, and in a friendly way asked his driver to bring in his kit. The reply was 'Aw, do it yourself.' PC and I looked at each other, but said nothing: their teams had their own individualistic ways of getting along. After a good chat – they had had no contact with fellow countrymen for weeks – the officer was dying to play bridge. Though reluctant, as I had only played a little family bridge, I made up the four. At the stakes he got us to accept (I had previously played for matches) it proved to be an expensive session for me, but he drove off in a cheerful mood next day. In a letter PC mentioned that he came across him again on a post-war TA (Territorial Army) exercise. His name was John Bramley.

As a nineteen-year-old I was involved in two incidents on the same day which could have had diplomatic repercussions. A party of Italian soldiers turned up at the crossroads where I was standing. They had been trapped in the country since September 1943, and made impassioned appeals for help to get them home. Despite the intensity of their dissatisfaction, I had to explain that there was little that we could do to assist in such matters, which had to remain in the hands of the Partisans. That evening, when I was walking by myself along a lonely stretch of road, a croaking voice came from nowhere. I looked around the featureless plain, and then realised that it must have come from the ditch. Two bearded and bedraggled figures pleaded with me in broken English to smuggle them out of the country. Despite their desperate plight, I had no option but to tell them that neither politically nor practically were we in a position to help Cetniks. All I could do was to show them on my map the Partisan locations that I knew about, and to wish them luck; an inadequate but inevitable course.

When I heard that 300 Germans were being held not far from Bileca, I went across to see how they were being treated. They were in large roofless buildings exposed to the elements, but that was the case for all of us much of the time. Many of them had greatcoats, and they seemed to be in reasonable shape. A German officer who spoke a little English said that their main worry was about getting enough food. Mainly through sign language I found out from the Partisans that some sheep had been allocated. These I had slaughtered and cooked, and I stayed to make sure that they all had that meal at least. Unhappy times.

Typical of limestone country, the Trebisnica emerges as a fully fledged river from the base of a cliff at Logor, just south of Bileca. I wandered down there with a couple of Marines, and we decided to use Mills bombs to see if we could get some fresh fish. After we had no luck from theirs, I lobbed mine, but I was too hearty, and it landed on the far bank. Two seconds later, metal fragments whizzed and hummed past our ears. Thank heavens none of us was hit. This time it was I who had to make the apologies. My sixth close encounter with 'friendly' fire – my own!

After my failure to reduce the Troop strength we moved back to Niksic. The Partisans had managed to blow the bridge at Bioce, about ten miles north-east of Pogdorica, so units of 21st Mountain Corps were building up in the town, making it a good target for BAF bombing when the weather permitted. PC was tasked to carry out a recce to see if an attack was possible to destroy the bridge repairs with further demolitions. This involved a long and arduous journey over the mountains lasting several days, so he briefed me on administrative points for taking over the Troop, and I wished him luck. As he was buckling on his equipment he casually added, 'By the way, fifty mules will be arriving this afternoon, and you'll have to get supplies to an LRDG patrol at this map reference (about twenty-five miles away).' I felt that this was a pretty cool test of my initiative considering that my animal experience was limited to a fox terrier. With a grin he wished *me* luck as he left. To my profound relief four Italians accompanied the mules, one of whom was a vet who spoke a little English. Between us we somehow found suitable quarters for the animals, and the three muleteers saw to their maintenance. The Italians gave us one day of instruction on how to fit harnesses and pack saddles, and in loading, leading, haltering and feeding. Then we set off on our own, using the Cyrillic map for the cross-country journey. At one stage we had to cross a rough bridge over a stream, and there was some delay before Sergeant George rejoined us. I asked him what the problem had been, and he said that his mule refused to cross water. 'However, I'd noticed that he was a bit lame in his left hind leg so I gave him a kick there, and he went over.' A pragmatic Derbyshire solution. Stevens's mule turned awkward, and kept shedding its load, so for one spell he ended up carrying a large carton of compo. There is nothing like necessity to get the hang of things, and the LRDG were grateful for the replenishments. On the journey back we felt like old hands at the game. Here are some notes that I jotted down – always water mules before feeding; have two full fodder bags per animal when leaving base; if mules scatter, put those that remain in a bunch, and the others will come in.

After that we learned how to handle the five loads into which 75mm mountain guns break down, and established a reputation for getting guns and supplies to difficult locations. The large mules carried the heavy, awkward loads: gun barrel, breech, wheels and so forth. The heavy barrel had to be hoisted by four men, who then moved forward alongside the hindquarters of the mule to lower it on to a wooden cradle, where it was lashed firm. Even so, this particularly awkward load always swung precariously when the mule had to struggle over rough ground, and we were constantly having to steady it. The breech block nestled more snugly above the wheels on either side of a pack. Restive animals could be quite a problem. Smaller mules took five 75mm shells in carriers on each side, or fodder, or boxes of compo rations. Saddles, once fitted, were marked for a numbered mule. When roads could be used to get us closer to objectives, six mules travelled head to tail in Dodge trucks. On a couple of occasions the Commander of Floydforce, Brigadier Pat O'Brien-Twohig DSO, came across us. He had a distinguished record as a Battalion Commander in the Royal Inniskilling Fusiliers. I stepped away from the necks of the mules I was leading to snap up salutes, and after friendly chats with us it was obvious that our activities appealed to him. He was a stocky Irishman with a broad face and bushy moustache, and in his caubeen with its green hackle he looked a bit of a brigand, albeit a smartly dressed one.

The Italian vet, whose name was Federico Tamburnotti, was the key figure in looking after the detachment, an excellent man. I have the tattered remains of the daily forage scale: barley or oats – 8 pounds; local hay or tibben or straw – 11 pounds; salt – 2 oz; carob beans for sick animals – 2 pounds. Our vet seemed to obtain over the odds on carob. The pods grow on trees in the eastern Mediterranean, starting off green and ripening to black. I came across them in Cyprus on Sandhurst exercises after the war, and again in Crete. It was with the mules that I learned the true meaning of 'getting one's oats' – all ears went up when the grain appeared. One big black beast of uncertain temperament and rolling eye we called Mussolini. There were two horses, which we rode with blankets on their backs, as there were only pack saddles. On exercise walks the mules never let the horses get ahead.

When PC got back from his recce he reported that the Bioce bridge area was very strongly defended, and that a troop attack would stand no chance at all. We were spared the long march and the likelihood of getting killed.

I cannot say that our role as muleteer troop had a profound influence on the strategic situation in Yugoslavia, but the training was to stand me in good stead when I took the first pioneer Brathay Expedition to south-west Greenland in 1967, when we hired ponies to carry our food, camping gear and scientific equipment inland to the Eqalorutsit glacier. Luckily I had borrowed three Army pack saddles and baggage equipment from a mule detachment at Aldershot, as the Greenlanders' saddles turned out to be bits of board attached to a girth strap, with string to go under the horses' tails! Attempts to load eight ponies in steady drizzle became a nightmare. There was little to tie on to, and everything depended on balance. Each time we carefully constructed a balanced load it rolled over when tested. The Army saddles had strong iron hooks and the baggage ropes had metal rings sewn in, so the lashed loads could be clipped on on both sides. Crossing the mountain terrain in bad weather with visibility reduced to fifteen yards led to dramatic incidents, but we achieved all our aims.

C Troop went on another escort operation which clearly illustrates the hidden political influences behind relations with the Partisans. Brigadier O'Brien-Twohig suggested that the guns should be employed to shell the enemy concentrations in Podgorica. It took ten days for authorisation to come through from Belgrade. The same force retraced its steps back to Risan, and then continued through Kotor and Cetinje, the former capital of the old kingdom of Montenegro, to get to a position south-west of Podgorica. Bad weather made the steep, narrow, winding roads very difficult for the heavy 25-pounders to negotiate. Bob Loudoun's blow had been repaired, but beyond that the

Germans had destroyed a bridge over a stream that was in full spate. After a prolonged argument with a Partisan engineer, our Sappers put a Bailey bridge across. Farther on, the incessant rain had caused a landslide. Partisans assisted them in clearing it, but the long column was beleaguered for another night. On 9 December 1944 the guns finally came within range. A signal came through from Floydforce HQ in Niksic that Partisan Command had given approval for the bombardment to open up in the morning. After the tribulations on the road the officers in the force were entertained to a good dinner at the Grand Hotel in Cetinje by Major Dalkovic, commander of the local Primorska Partisans. Very cordial relations had been established when Colonel Jago, the Gunner Commander, received another signal: 'Previous signal cancelled. All forward movement stopped. Concentrate all forces Viluse 10 Dec.'

At first light the guns and vehicles took up their places once more and wound slowly back again on a round journey of over 180 miles. Jago was told that Podgorica was on the verge of falling, and that the guns were needed to counter a new threat from Mostar. He became a deeply suspicious man. This was typical – good relations at the local level were thwarted by devious ploys at the top. The Germans did not move out from Podgorica until the night of 18–19 December – ten days later – and Mostar was a great many miles away.

General Vukanovic, the Montenegrin Commander, authorised another proposal. This was to lift a Troop of RSR guns with a Commando escort by air from Niksic airstrip to a Partisan-held strip at Berane, east of Kolasin, to impede the retreat to the north. 'Flagerforce' was commanded by Major Neil Munro, our second-in-command, and A Troop was nominated as escort. If the enemy strength became too strong the force would escape into Albania. The transport planes were Dakotas and Italian Savoias, and they had much trouble in working out loading tables for the latter. On 6 December 1944 they actually emplaned. This time the weather intervened – the start of that seven-day spell of rain and low cloud. By the end of that period the Germans were moving through in such strength that the operation had to be cancelled.

On 11 December word came through that the Germans had pulled out of Davilovgrad (the *Official History* states that German engineers had rebridged the Bioce gap by 10 December). I must have been within easy range of Commando HQ as I was called in and told to recce the road down the Zeta valley and report on its state for taking guns. I drove up by jeep as far as I could, and then proceeded on foot. The road was embanked out from the mountainside, and at the head of the valley the Partisans had blown gaps to prevent an advance on Niksic. Lower down the Germans had done the same to cover their retreat. It was difficult to scramble across the rubble on the steep slopes, and having done this eight or nine times I went back and reported that repairs would take over a week (the *History* states that there were thirty-one demolitions along the whole route). The Partisans displayed remarkable

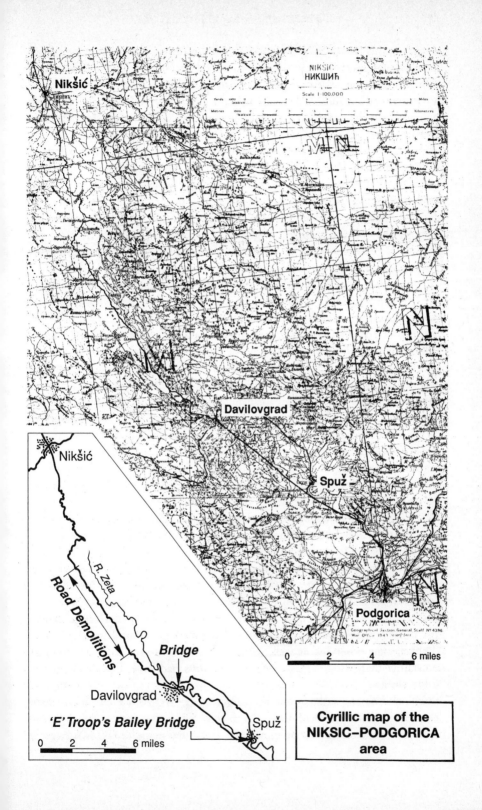

Nikšić

Davilovgrad

Spuž

Podgorica

NIKSIĆ
НИКШИЋ

Scale 1:100,000

Geographical Section General Staff Nº 4396
War Office 1943

0   2   4   6 miles

Nikšić

R. Zeta

Road Demolitions

Bridge

Davilovgrad

Spuž

'E' Troop's Bailey Bridge

0   2   4   6 miles

Cyrillic map of the
NIKSIC–PODGORICA
area

administrative ability and determination in rounding up every able-bodied man, woman and child from Niksic to work on the road southward, and the same was done from Danilovgrad northward. Every available Commando and Gunner joined in, and Sappers instructed us on how to set about things. Again there was friendly cameraderie at our worker level, and genuine dedication on the part of the Yugoslavs. Their zeal – many of them worked with bare hands – opened up the road after three days of hard work. On 13 December a Battery of 25-pounders and a Troop of RSR 75s edged their way forward, with each gun supported by a working party – we chocked the wheels with stones as we went along. They reached Danilovgrad, and opened up on the 14th. OPs reported that the unexpected shelling caused much panic and confusion amongst the retreating forces. Two days later the 3.7 inch HAA guns got through. They were lethal in a ground role, and extended the range. Finally another battery of 25-pounders added to the barrage on the 16th.

The last rearguard pulled back from Spuz on the night of 15–16 December, and E Troop arrived there on the 16th. This was the only time that I got close to the Germans during our three months on the mainland. A stone bridge in Davilovgrad had been destroyed, but Sappers had overcome that problem. The smaller bridge near Spuz was blown on the 15th, so that was the last gap preventing the guns from following up the retreat. Three Sappers were available, E Troop provided the unskilled labour, and Bailey bridge equipment appeared with a speed that surprised me at the time. Mike McConville's book *A Small War in the Balkans* (he was in C Troop) tells how it was recovered from the coast, where it had been used on their second abortive trip. A German OP had been left on the high escarpment overlooking Spuz, and every time we ventured out to the river bank, shells came down which were too close for comfort. Construction had to be done at night. Bolting the sections together was straightforward, but the system of rollers and counterweights to launch it was technical stuff. We shoved and heaved and shoved and heaved as the Sappers made adjustments. Finally it worked, and the forward section reached the other side. It is tremendously satisfying to have built a bridge. D Troop immediately went across to set up defensive positions. A good night's work. During the heavy shelling which continued throughout the next day we were as anxious for the bridge as we were for our own skins. There were no direct hits, and that night the Germans pulled back out of range. It was now our Gunners who established OPs on the high ground, and they had a light aircraft observing as well, so this second Floydforce contact was more devastating than the first. 21st Mountain Corps had moved out of range by 24 December.

Gunner officers walked over the target areas, and found out how much destruction the shelling had done. On the ground one sees the pointless loss of life, whereas the strategists are concerned as to how many divisions survive to be deployed on other fronts. It was as well that we were young and took things as they came, without introspection.

I walked into Podgorica, which was a scene of desolation. Hardly a building remained intact. Rubble was everywhere, and smoke still rose from smouldering fires after the heavy bombing. It was the Balkan Air Force sorties which inflicted the greatest damage on the retreat. They also dropped leaflets urging the Germans to surrender, some of which we picked up. Here and there a few shabbily dressed, silent figures searched through the ruins. Most of the population had fled to the hills: there would be little comfort for them when they returned. The town was later rebuilt as Titograd. I met a fearsome group of guerrillas with long hair, black beards, unkempt uniforms, bandoliers, grenades and pistols. After establishing that they were Albanians, language difficulties did not take us much further.

The Commando returned to Niksic for Christmas, which was bitterly cold, with snow on the ground. Most of them enjoyed a dinner in the State Opera House, followed by a concert. E Troop went back to our farmhouse and our mules. PC had been hoarding his NAAFI ration of spirits for some time, and produced enough for everyone in the Troop to have a good measure of whisky. He and I did the traditional thing of waiting on the men, and although there were few culinary frills we had a convivial evening. In the morning I found an Army Form C2136 (small) pinned to my blankets with a pencilled 'Merry Xmas Jenky. Your snack is coming up in a 3 Tonner. Slack, Jack and Whack [the three sergeants] and the Sergeant Major'. Just the message form: nothing more.

On 29 December we returned to Dubrovnik. Over the next three weeks we had to show the greatest restraint. The Partisans imposed strict curfews, barred us from Dubrovnik without special permission (we were back in the timber yard near Gruz), and closed wine bars to us. These are not things that fighting soldiers take to kindly when they have come back from testing and frustrating conditions in the field, but on the whole the men behaved well, and accepted the need to ignore insults. A corporal in E Troop, who shall be nameless, was a lad for the ladies, so PC gave him dire warnings. His secretive behaviour at times made me wonder if he was achieving his ambition, but if so he kept it concealed from the Partisans as well, and there was no major incident.

The Communist commissars did their best to prevent contact between us and the civilians. As a tourist resort before the war, Dubrovnik had profited from capitalists spending their money, and historic ties between Montenegro and Serbia had been close, so many people favoured restoration of the monarchy.

Inevitably the Partisans did arrest some of our men, but not on any serious charges, and we were able to secure their release. I was involved in one such incident when I was Garrison Duty Officer on 5 January 1945. The following

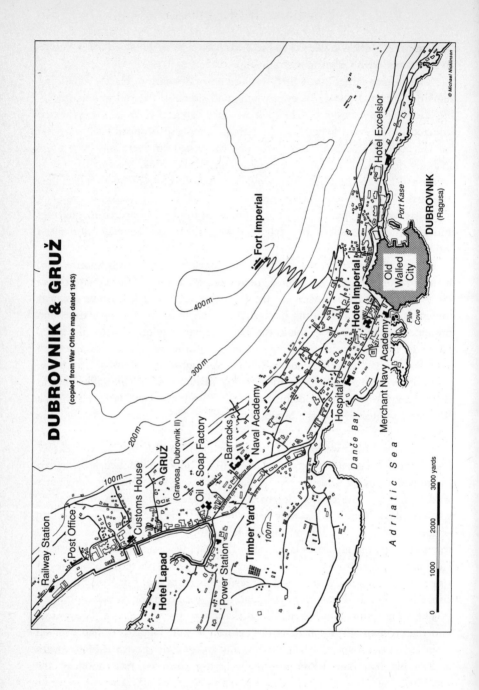

DUBROVNIK & GRUŽ

(copied from War Office map dated 1943)

Railway Station

Post Office

Customs House

GRUŽ
(Gravosa, Dubrovnik II)

Oil & Soap Factory

Barracks

Naval Academy

Hotel Lapad

Power Station

Timber Yard

100m

100m

200m

300m

400m

Fort Imperial

Hospital

Hotel Imperial

Merchant Navy Academy

Danče Bay

Adriatic Sea

Pile Cove

Old Walled City

Port Kase

Hotel Imperial

Hotel Excelsior

DUBROVNIK
(Ragusa)

© Michael Nicklinson

0   1000   2000   3000 yards

are notes that I jotted down in my Field Message Book. Not all of them would have been included verbatim in my final report!

0900   Mount guard.

0915   Collect mail.

0930   Reported to Adjt. Read Orders.
Visited Mule Lines – 30 out on exercise; 12 saddled by 1100; 2 mules not to be saddled: one with wound under fore-belly, one with rump graze and hock wound; 1 mule with head sore – no head harness; 6 mules need shoeing. Checked the inventories with Pte Chandler. 1 Dressing Tray deficient and 1 thermometer broken in Veterinary Chest.

1115   Billet and Galley [Cookhouse] Rounds.

1215   Visit to Brigade HQ. My report to go to the DAQMG. Contacted the Liaison Officer about Eyties pay and passes. Deciphered their names.

1230   Dinner Rounds.

1400   Drew NAAFI supplies for E Troop muleteers and attached soldiers,
to   and for the remainder of E Troop in the Timber Yard. Went round to
1600   issue them, and collected money from each person – 75 all told.
Raining. Jeep to take out Petrol Guards.
Mounted single-banked sentries on each dump.
Visited DID. [I doubt if I knew what this abbreviation stood for at the time, but I have recently been informed that it was Detail Issue Depot]. Received phone reports from all units in the Garrison (111 Field Regt RA; 180 HAA Regt RA; 2825 RAF Regt; 514 Coy, RASC; 479 Field Coy, RE; Signals detachment; 150 Coy, Pioneer Corps; Beach Group, RN; DID; Medical Section, CRS; Movements).
Passed them on to the Staff Captain at Brigade HQ.
Started to write my report, but the lights failed.
Just got my books off to turn in when there was a phone call. Clr Sgt Parker, Duty NCO of F Troop, was trying to bail out six chaps from Jug arrest. Went in the jeep to a house half-way down the hill leading into Dubrovnik. Discussed the situation as best I could with the Jug sentries – solid bastards. Eventually saw Dubrovnik Garrison Commander, Col Bogdan, inside the town. Told Bogdan that he would have to produce witnesses and an interpreter to substantiate any case that our men had assaulted a Partisan. Foxed him when we spoke in French, and managed to persuade him not to send off a signal to his HQ. Signed for the men, and got them out just after midnight. One Marine was drunk and improperly dressed, so he was placed under

close arrest and taken to the guardroom. The Cpl and four Marines were placed under open arrest for breaking out of camp and being absent without leave. It was well after 0100 before I got to bed.

6 Jan. 45

0730   Took a 3-Tonner with a Cpl and three Marines from the guard to pick up 300 jerrycans. Raining hard. Dropped off 37 at each galley. Late breakfast. Should have attended the Court Martial to learn about it, but had to appear as witness for Jack Bolton's investigation into the charges against his men. Attended CO's Orderly Room when they came up in front of Neil Munro. I expect he contacted Col Bogdan and told him how he'd dealt with them. Went up to the Mule Lines to give Sgt George the detail for the day. Sorted out the NAAFI money (£17.15.6), and handed it in. Wrote a full report on the night's proceedings, and took it to Brigade HQ.

My copy of the Daily Orders has survived, and they give an idea of day-to-day administration.

Garrison Duty SNCO
He will muster the Tobacco Factory Fatigue Party consisting of 9 ORs of all units billeted there at 0900 hrs, and will supervise the cleaning up of the stairways, entrance hall, ledge facing road, and rear courtyard of the Tobacco Factory.

Barrack Discipline
Reports have been received of troops lighting fires in the Tobacco Factory. This dangerous practice will cease immediately.

Fatigue Party
Sigs Section and 'I' Section will parade outside Hotel ZAGREB daily at 0830 hrs. Dress loose order under Clr Sgt PARKER for cleaning up Hotel ZAGREB.

Engineering Course
Ranks detailed for Engineering Course will parade at QM's Store, TIMBER YARD at 0800 hrs tomorrow under Sgt ABRAMS. Further instructions re course will be issued by Lieut J.P. STEVENS.

FGCM (Field General Court Martial)
A FGCM will be held in VILLA EDEN, LAPAD at 1030 hrs Sat 6 Jan. Sgt SEDDON will carry out duties of Court Orderly.

Dental Treatment
All available ranks of B, D, E and HQ Troops will be marched to the Hospital, GRUZ, to arrive there at 1400 hrs tomorrow for Dental inspection.

Training Conference

There will be a Training Conference at 1430 hrs tomorrow 6 Jan. at the Officers Mess. All Troop Cmd, all HQ Officers, and the RSM will attend.

D F ESSON
Lieut and A/Adjt

Neil Munro had become acting CO when Ian MacAlpine was invalided home. MacAlpine had served in the First World War, and had previously been CO of 6 Commando in Tunisia. He was the only Army Officer (Black Watch) to command a RM Commando. Our new CO, Ian Riches, took over in the middle of November when we were widely dispersed in Montenegro. As a pre-war Regular he dealt with the problems in Dubrovnik by keeping us fully occupied with training and physical exercise. Just behind Dubrovnik a very steep road zig-zags up to Fort Imperial, 1250 feet up. Pounding up and down we got to know it well. We were back to target shooting, engineer courses, and the handling of enemy weapons.

One evening at dusk I was driving up round the bends of the coastal road when I noticed flashes ahead. There was a captured German lorry in front, with Partisans in the back. Suddenly I realised that they were tossing hand grenades out just for the hell of it, so I did not get too close.

I had an unpleasant reminder of this careless attitude when I took a Brathay expedition to Planina polje in Slovenia in 1960. Jurij Kunaver, a geography lecturer from Ljubljana university who helped us with our field work, and I were entering a village one day when there was a loud bang, which I instantly recognised as a grenade explosion. A plume of white smoke rose from a nearby courtyard. We rushed in. A small girl of about seven was lying with her leg almost severed at the knee though, like the airmen, there was no blood. I had just cradled her in my arms when her eyes rolled, and she was gone. A small boy had withstood the shock, but his leg was a bloody mess. While we applied a tourniquet he watched without making a sound: a tough little chap. By this time the courtyard was full of wailing villagers, and Jurij told them to get a blanket and to call an ambulance quickly. I was greatly saddened but not surprised when he wrote to say that the boy had to lose his leg. Loss of life in wartime has to be accepted, but for the lives of small children to be shattered fifteen years later was shocking. Civil war has subjected civilians to death and anguish yet again. It is tragic that the bitter internal disputes have re-emerged now that Tito is dead and Communism has been overthrown. The factional grudges and prejudices are feudal and emotional and too many people in former Yugoslavia are as tough, stubborn and intransigent as ever. The only consistent thread in Balkan history has been bloody-mindedness in both the literal and the metaphorical sense.

On 20 January 1945 LCIs took us off, and we sailed away from Yugoslavia with no regrets. It is only now that I have formed a cohesive picture of this period. The Troops were isolated from one another for the most part, and one only knew what was going on in the local area. Except for C Troop nothing much happened for most of the time. When we met up again at Dubrovnik we gained a rough idea of what the others had been doing, but it was anecdotal. We certainly had no idea of what had been going on at the top or behind the scenes.

Partisan priorities had changed from hitting the enemy as hard as possible to making sure that an independent Communist regime would be set up in all parts of the country. An additional objective was to reclaim the province of Venezia Giulia, which had been part of the Austrian Empire before Italy annexed it after the First World War. The Partisan Fourth Army by-passed towns in Croatia and Slovenia still occupied by the Germans and headed straight for Trieste. They arrived there on 1 May 1945, one day before General Freyberg's New Zealand Second Division entered the city. The situation became extremely tense, as the Allies were not prepared to allow Tito to take control of Trieste, with its predominantly Italian population. This was the first East–West confrontation, which developed into the Cold War. (See Franklin Lindsay's book *Beacons in the Night*. Lindsay became head of the American Mission to Tito.)

CHAPTER 6

Italy: In the Front Line

We were given a few days off in Bari, so I booked in at the Officers' Club in the Imperiale Hotel. The luxury of a hot bath after three months – and clean sheets to sleep in! Not to mention well-cooked meals after the constant diet of Army biscuits and compo. Hard living helps one to appreciate the simpler things of life. From 8–23 February 1945 we were in the bleak mountains around Minervino carrying out intensive training in conventional warfare to prepare us for the front line. Then came four days in cattle trucks for a slow journey up to Ravenna, where we went into billets. The town had been captured by the Canadians on 4 December 1944 so the civilians were still intrigued by the change from German to Allied occupation. A pretty young Italian girl rode her bicycle fast up and down in front of a group of us giving a most provocative smile, and her light frock billowed high up on her thighs. As an officer I just watched, but she got a vociferous response from the Marines before I took them off on their duties.

2 Commando arrived just before us, on 14 February, and 9 Commando and 40 RM Commando turned up in the middle of March. Three Army officers, Douglas Cotton-Minchin, John Page and Stan Barnes, and a CS Captain, 'Shorty' Roberts, were posted in to 43. Within two months all four were killed or wounded. Brigadier Ronnie Tod, former CO of 9 Commando, had taken over from Tom Churchill, and V Corps HQ had to help us out, as we were much more lightly equipped than an Infantry Brigade. They provided us with transport, and supply problems were soon fixed, so it was only a few days before we were committed to the line. One great improvement was that we handed in our ancient jerkins, and were issued with parachute smocks instead. The long front zip enabled us to be cooler or snug, and the numerous large pockets were ideal for stowing all the things required on night patrols.

(After digging out the maps I have been surprised how close the forward positions were to Ravenna – only seven and a half miles to the north-west.) On the approach roads we came across famous divisional signs of Eighth Army units which had fought their way across North Africa and up from the toe of Sicily – the Black Hat, Mailed Fist, Battle-Axe, Desert Rat. The Commando was back to a formal Army environment after the many months of independent operations.

At the beginning of March, E Troop occupied Sector C, just beyond the ferry across the River Lamone. Our left flank was the N16 road. The 12th

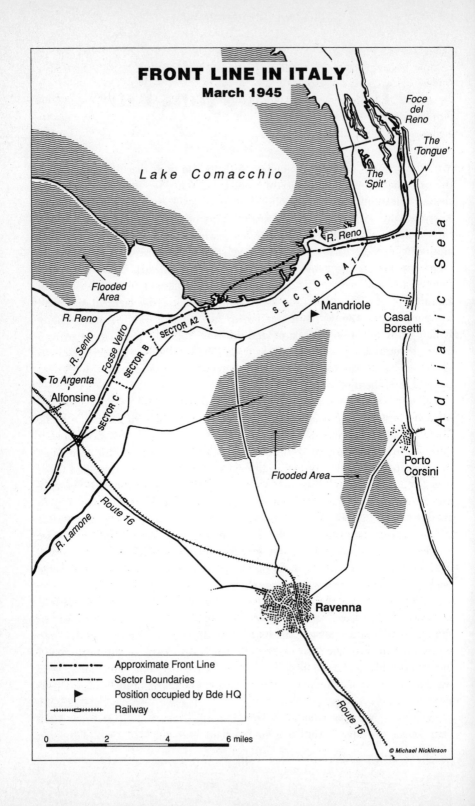

FRONT LINE IN ITALY
March 1945

Foce del Reno

The 'Tongue'

Lake Comacchio

The 'Spit'

R. Reno

Flooded Area

SECTOR A1

Mandriole

Casal Borsetti

R. Reno

R. Senio

Fosse Vetro

SECTOR A2

SECTOR B

SECTOR C

To Argenta

Alfonsine

Porto Corsini

Flooded Area

R. Lamone

Route 16

Adriatic Sea

Ravenna

Route 16

–··–·–·–·	Approximate Front Line
·–··–··–··	Sector Boundaries
▶	Position occupied by Bde HQ
┼┼┼┼┼┼┼┼	Railway

0   2   4   6 miles

© Michael Nicklinson

Lancers were in support with three Churchills and a Honey tank, and F Troop's 3-inch Mortar section was also attached. During the take-over, night guides took us forward, in my case to the Casa di Metza farmhouse, with half the Troop. The line had been static for a couple of months, so it was real First World War stuff – forward Bren positions with covered approaches were occupied on a relief system; no movement by day for the rest of us; full stand-to at dusk and dawn. No-man's-land was completely flat, and consisted of vineyards and drainage ditches, with some scattered orchard trees. Five hundred yards away the German forward positions were dug through the far bank of the Fosso Vetro canal, east of Alfonsine. Like us they lived in farmhouses to give cover for cooking and sleeping, in their case Casa Morini, Casa Riccibitti and Casa Tosca, which were close to the canal.

At night I took out patrols up to our bank of the canal to guard against any incursions. We had to be careful as mines had been laid by both the Germans and the Canadians, so we kept to safe routes. In the take-over briefing I was told that the Germans had a fixed line on the track leading up to my farmhouse. This meant that there was a Spandau set up on a tripod, and if a sentry got bored all he had to do was to reach up and press the trigger. On the occasions when I had to go out and back there was always the uneasy expectation of a burst of bullets, but fortunately they did not materialise.

Casa di Metza had bare but solidly built stone walls inside and out. There was an upper storey formerly occupied by the family, and the animals had been stalled in the ground-floor area. For added protection this is where we now lived. The cows had been killed by the shelling. By this time the carcases, half-buried in the rubble in the yard, had swelled ominously and their skins were taut. During my recce of the building I noticed that there was daylight between the wall and the eaves of the roof in one corner. After scouting around I came across a ladder, which I took upstairs. The narrow gap provided an excellent observation position, and I spent a good deal of time trying to detect enemy movement through my binoculars, but they remained holed up just as we did. Water was scarce, and had to be boiled or sterilised with tablets. One mug was allowed for individual wash, shave and cleaning of teeth, and one basin per section for wipe-downs.

We were on the ground floor as usual when one morning there was a deafening explosion, and the whole farmhouse shook. After the dust and debris had settled I went upstairs. There was a gaping hole at my OP, and the top four rungs of the ladder had been blown away. It was a lucky shot to have landed bang on target, but most impressive. The German observer must have been dancing a jig. He had probably picked up the sun glinting on my binoculars. From now on it was to be close encounters with enemy fire. For some reason the Germans were restive that day. Another shell landed two feet away from the stable wall, and others went over to the right rear and on to the tank track.

Then in the evening there was Nebelwerfer and rifle-grenade fire from their front line positions, but no one was hit.

Our first relief was by a Palestinian battalion of the Jewish Brigade. They were obviously very efficient and eager to get at the Germans, as they questioned me closely about their positions. When we got back we found that they had stirred things up with aggressive fighting patrols. As a result we were subjected to heavier shelling: luckily not for long, as we were moved to another sector before we had any casualties, and before the carcases burst.

I still have the small piece of paper on which PC scribbled some notes about the next hand-over. He sent them across by runner, as he was unable to contact me on our field telephone. They are not in official format, but their message, as usual, was clear:

J. 1. You will be relieved by a party of 18 ITALIAN PARTISANS at about 2045 tonight.

   2. Get all your stores out of your casa as soon as poss after dark.

   3. Think out posns for 18 men (tactics don't matter, get them each a hole) and place them yourself, pointing out the direction of the TEDESCHI [Italian for Germans].

   4. Get all your men and stores back here as quickly as poss. Bring spare Bren, water-cans, and all other gear except gash [naval slang for spare food], if any. Bring PHONE, even though Ites have none.

   5. Ites occupy house at rd junc LOCONOVO so be ready for challenge. I shall be with them to stop them shooting you.

   6. Bring stores to where jeep dropped them last night at my casa, and leave them.

   7. Take your chaps straight on to Tac HQ, and fit them into any transport available, which will take them to the billet in RAVENNA.

   8. Try and get through on the phone if you have any questions, we can't get you.

   9. Repeat, get away as fast as you can.   RNPC

Our stay in Ravenna was brief, as next night we had a rotten journey in the dark up to Sector A1, and did not doss down in the rear area until 0330. In the morning PC and I went forward to recce the new Commando front, which extended 6000 yards inland from the Adriatic coast. This is where we were to launch the curtain raiser for the Eight Army's spring offensive. The two of us must have been spotted as we walked back, as we were stonked by 88mm shells just as we reached an orchard. E Troop was on the extreme left, and this time we were less than seventy yards from the enemy. Both sides had tunnelled through the dykes, and dugouts faced each other across the River Reno. During the night, occupation carrying parties had a wearying time trudging back and forth four times over a long approach route to get our food, water, ammunition and signals batteries forward. We relieved the Gurkhas, and I was most impressed by the thoroughness of the corporal who briefed me. We crawled forward to all the slit trenches and from each one he pointed out the German positions and told me what had happened over the last twenty-four hours. Then he made me repeat everything to satisfy himself that I had understood his English. I set sentries, and organised watches.

As before most of us holed up by day in *casas* well back from the river, and only the men manning the Bren-guns and the snipers were forward in the dugouts. Beale, using telescopic sights, claimed two certain kills, and told us the facial details of his victims. One evening a heavy 105mm self-propelled gun selected my *casa* as its target. I was standing in the downstairs area, and the off-duty Marines were sitting with their backs against the wall a few feet in front of me when there was a heavy thud outside. It was not long before a much louder explosion occurred just behind the farmhouse. Then came an almighty bang, and the 2 ft-thick stone wall cracked open in front of my eyes. Tipton's webbing was hanging on a nail and it fell on his head, split in two. He must have been slightly shell-shocked as for the next hour or so he kept exclaiming in an astonished voice that his equipment was unwearable. Corporal Jackson, Sugden and Pillinger had minor lacerations from flying chips of stone which I cleaned and bound up from the first aid haversack. Four or five more shells fell close, but gradually we became less keyed up as the period of silence lengthened. It takes some time to feel safe again.

After I had posted the sentries I decided to remain on watch. German gunners continued to dog me as they bombarded our sector of the dyke with uncomfortable accuracy. Marine Flyn and I huddled in the bottom of our dugout, hoping that it would not receive a direct hit. One shell fell short in the river and we both got drenched by the spray. I chose the wrong night to do my stint!

Next day we surveyed the scene around the farmhouse. The first shell had landed in the manure heap, hence the thud. Luckily for us the direct hit burst on the foundations of a solid section of wall between two windows. If it had been a couple of feet higher I would not be writing this. Other craters were scattered around the yard. When we took over we had dug heads (latrines) in a covered position outside. We discovered that we had to dig new ones much sooner than expected: the first ones were considerably enlarged.

I went across to D Troop's positions further to the right. They had twenty dead mules lying near their *casa*, and German equipment was still scattered around. Some of the animals had burst or been hit so the atmosphere was none too salubrious. One of our Bren groups had been detached to A Troop in the woods south of the Tongue, the spit of land east of the mouth of the Reno, so I continued on to dish out their NAAFI rations.

A group of Partisans from 28 Garibaldi Brigade, with their distinctive bright red neck-scarves, came to relieve us so that we could have a day's rest in the rear area. Here there was another First World War touch – a Mobile Bath Unit. The portly middle-aged major in charge was much impressed by the green berets, and we were treated as heroes, which was an amusing boost to our egos. After the skimpy wipe-downs we revelled in the streams of hot water cascading down our bodies. Sheer luxury to soap all over, and to cap it all we were each given clean underwear and socks to put on afterwards. A great institution. When we returned to our front-line positions that night we had to wake up half the Italians; their kit was all over the place, and they straggled off leaving bits and pieces behind. What a contrast to the Gurkhas.

After flowing eastward just south of Lake Comacchio, the Reno bends north for the last three miles, leaving the tongue of land east of its mouth. In the planned attack, Operation 'Roast', we had to capture this enemy-held territory, so we sent out no less than nineteen patrols to probe their defences. Captain Douglas Cotton-Minchin of the Cameronians had been an instructor at Achnacarry when I was there on my course. On the night of 15 March he took out a patrol from B Troop to ambush an enemy mine-laying party. He advanced ahead of his men; fire broke out from a German position, and that was the last that was seen of him. The Marines had great difficulty in extricating themselves, and two of them found that they had bullet-holes in their uniforms when they got back. Douglas was posted as missing, but we hoped that he had been taken prisoner. Sadly there was no trace, so after the war he was declared 'Dead with no known grave'. Awful for his family.

On 18–19 March it was my turn. Neil Munro handed me my orders, told me to read them, and then went through them carefully on the maps and air photos. I could tell by the look in his eyes that he was reluctant to have to do this, and that he felt that he was likely to lose another officer. There were good grounds for this anxiety, as I was prone to take a chance, but when I crawled forward on my own my luck was in, as the enemy trench was not occupied at the time. PC read through my report when I got back and added map references. I wrote out another copy to send to Brigade HQ, so I still have my original draft, which I have prefaced by some details from the operation order:

This order will NOT be carried by the patrol

3. **Object**
   Recce patrol to observe and report on enemy minefields, defences and movement in area 636582.

5. **Sp Fire** (supporting fire).

(shelling before we left)	{	142 Regt HF Arty 1800–1845 Target RF12 to include airbursts
	{	1845–1900 Target DF1123
	{ 56 Bty	HF Arty 1800–1900 Target area RONCONI
	{	632573
(available to help to get us out of trouble)	{	Arty and Mortars on call for targets from 1900
	{	X-639578; Y-638577; Z-639582; RF12-637584
	{	River Bank – Arty DF1123, Mortar DF8

6. **Sigs**

Call for Fire Targets X and Z – Two white Vereys

Y and RF12 – Two green Vereys

River Bank – Two red Vereys

7. **Security**

Men to be warned that the presence of Cdo personnel is to be kept secret in this sector.

8. **Med**

Two extra stretchers in A Troop area.

9. **Dress**

Denims or BD without flashes. No berets, smocks, or other means of identification of Cdo Tps will be worn. Minimum equipment.

10. **ADM**

Rum issue to be drawn at 1800 from F Troop HQ.

Report on Recce Patrol

Night 18/19 Mar 45   W G Jenkins Lt. RM

Strength   1 Offr   1 Cpl   3 Mnes

4 TSMG's (Thompson Sub Machine Guns) 5 mags a gun

Verey pistol. 6 cartridges.

1 '36' (Mills bomb)   1 smoke grenade per man.

Compass.

Information

1900   Left F Troop area.

1930   Arrived A Troop fwd posn.

1940   Taken by Lt. Haworth to the gap in the minefield.

Checked out with the LP [Listening Post] at the Tower.

Cut a telephone wire leading from the Tower to the German posns.

Gap in actual fact not a gap as we passed five box mines about ten feet out

Sketch Map for Patrol.

W. Jenkins.
Lt. R.M.

Half burned down house

Boat

Voices & Hammering of Stakes.

Furrows with small bushes
Coughing.
Small ditches
Road with back a ditch each side
Sound of boat?

Barschak posn 636582

Wooden uprights with wires.

Ronconi (figures silhouetted)

2 men lying in ditch.

Boa minefield

--- Route out
... " Back

Tower

CA p.

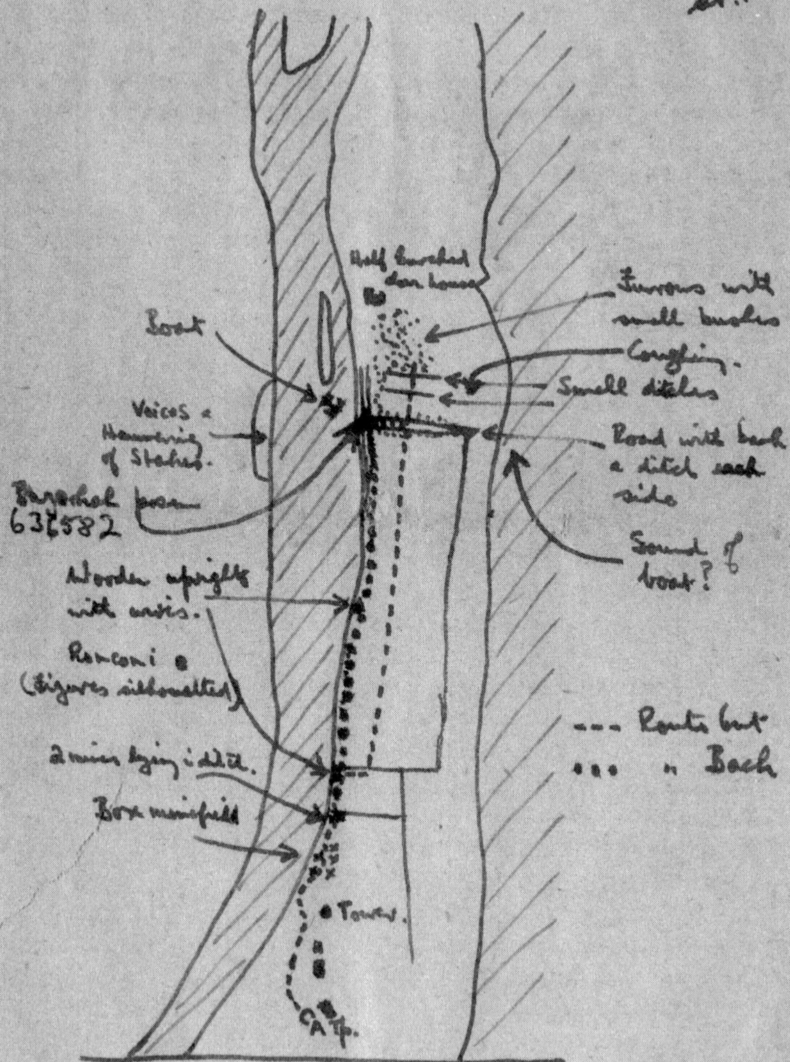

The ditch along the river bank on the route back does not give cover the whole way. as it flattens out in parts from the dyke. Easy enough to negotiate as all mines stand out clearly. One or two lids laid as dummies.

Depth of minefield about 20 yds. Two box mines in the ditch at the corner of the next dyke. These were not laid, and a crate was nearby. 636569.

Continued along the field just next to the river bank as far as the second dyke. 637571.

Moved 50 yds inland and advanced 800 yds up the large field, keeping 50 to 100 yds from the river bank.

Lay up at 636578 and listened. Only sounds heard were paddling or swishing of something in the water just up the river on the left. Also heard a cough from right, forward, but very difficult to place the exact position.

As everything was very quiet I decided to move forward. This we did in bounds of 100 yds, listening up in between, until we came to the dyke and road. 637582.

NO ENEMY OR POSITIONS AT TOP OF BIG FIELD.

Time reached 800 yd posn – 2200. Road – 2230.

At the end of the big field there is a low bank, then a ditch, then the road, then another bank and another ditch. Lay up on forward bank for some time. Once again heard a cough over on the right. Also a sound such as someone rowing, or pushing a wheelbarrow. Remarkably little sound on the spit itself – practically none except for one or two coughs and some indeterminate rustling on the right. [In this report 'spit' (geographically correct) refers to the tongue of land lying east of the mouth of the Reno. In Operation 'Roast', 'spit' refers to the seven-mile narrow band of land separating Lake Comacchio from the sea.] No voices. Voices were heard quite distinctly from the western bank of the river opposite the road. Also the sound of banging in stakes. Both about 634582. As no noise at all had been heard on the left hand side of the spit I decided to advance a bit further. Advanced 10 yds fwd, crossing two small ditches. The

Key to Sketch Map for Patrol (see facing page)

Left section, top to bottom: Boat. Voices and hammering of stakes. Bazookah [properly *Panzerfaust*] position 636582. Wooden upright with wires. Ronconi (figures silhouetted). Two mines lying in ditch. Box minefield.

Middle section, top to bottom: Half knocked down house. Tower. A Troop.

Right section, top to bottom: Furrows with small bushes. Coughing. Small ditches. Road with bank and ditch each side. Sound of a boat? – – – Route out ••• Route back

Below the sketch: The ditch along the river bank on the route back does not give cover the whole way as it flattens out in parts.

ground then became a bit rougher – furrows with little bushes on top of them. Went about ten yards in, and did not come across any mines or tripwires. Did not advance further as the cough had been heard abreast of us. Went back to the road and continued listening watch. 637583.

After a little time explored the road to the left. Found we had come out 100 yds from the river bank.

At the corner, 636582, came across an abandoned bazookah posn, containing: 3 Mausers, 2 Stick grenades, Spandau ammo drum, *Panzerfaust*, box of rifle-grenades [half normal, half a heavier A/Tk type], tin of Spandau ammo, and an eiderdown. [The Americans had an anti-tank weapon, the bazookah, which was also fired from on top of the shoulder, and this name instead of *Panzerfaust* came first to my mind when I was writing the report.]

Went about 20 yds up the road towards the house but found no Jerries. About 50 yds off-shore, 635583, saw what I at first thought was a boat with bodies in it, and then put down to be a small island not marked. Subsequently found out from Major Hudspith [A Troop commander] that it probably was a boat, and it may have caused the swishing we heard. In that case was quite large, and quite full, but they didn't make any noise.

The moon had gone in about 2330 and it was much darker. I therefore decided to recce the path along the river bank back. Did not see any more positions on the way back. There is a ditch on the inland side of the river bank track giving 4–5 ft cover if necessary, though we didn't have to use it, and walked along the track and the edge of the field.

Picked up a box of German mortar sights en route.

There are two lots of posts with thick plain wire between them along the track. These are firmly dug in, but are not mined. The wire is easy to get over, and the posts are easily visible, one about 636574, the second 300 yds south of it.

Saw figures silhouetted by the light of the haystack fires started by the arty in the area RONCONI. Roughly about ten. [Ronconi was on the west bank of the Reno]. Checked in with LP at Tower. Checked in with A Troop. Checked in with F Troop. Had a mortar stonk put down on RONCONI and X target on right of spit. Also arty on bank of river opposite the road.

Reported to Duty Officer.

Remarks. The ground is almost completely open except for shell holes and the dykes. The dark patches on the aerial photo for the big field were open patches of clayey mud without vegetation. From the listening it looks as if there are no enemy on the left side of the spit, probably as far as the house. Everything was extremely quiet there. Some Verey lights were going up from the western side of the river beyond the spit.

At 0730 on 19 March two 105 shells landed alongside the house and the blast burst through a window. I had just dossed down after rewriting my patrol report and did not bother to stir. We were relieved by 2 Commando as it was our turn to carry out the work-up for 'Roast'. I passed on my range-cards to Jerry Jermyn before we marched back to Mandriole, where transport was waiting for us. It took us straight through Ravenna to the training area at Sassi, where we bivouacked.

After briefing us on what we had to do, Ian Riches read out a commendation on our E Troop patrol which he had received from Brigadier Ronnie Tod. He raised a laugh when he said that several Germans must have been put on serious charges for losing equipment – we had brought back the Mausers, *Panzerfaust* and Mortar sights. For the next week we were hard at it practising river crossings and attacks on strongpoints. Some of us were allowed off one evening, so we took a jeep into Ravenna to see Ronald Colman and Jean Arthur in *Talk of the Town*.

Fantails (Landing Vehicles Tracked) were lightly armoured amphibious vehicles designed to cross flooded areas and to climb muddy banks. They had been used successfully in the Scheldt estuary in October 1944 when 41, 47 and 48 RM Commandos and 4 Commando took Walcheren after heavy fighting. Our Brigade tried them out for the first time in Italy. Kangaroos (Armoured Personnel Carriers) were converted Sherman tanks – the turrets and ammunition stowage were removed to allow room to carry soldiers, and they provided full protection on the move. Weasels were small tracked carriers, originally designed to tow sleds on snow. At Comacchio they were used to move Storm boats to the launching areas, which helped to ease the manpower effort. On one of our practice crossings of the River Uniti the amphibious adaptations to one of them did not work, and it sank. The crew baled out in time, but it presented the Royal Engineer Recovery Unit with a problem.

During the practice attacks on strongpoints we learned how to work with tanks and artillery in addition to our Heavy Weapons Troop. 'Shorty' Roberts had to catch up on infantry work, as he had only recently come ashore after a long period of sea service. His classic remark when he came across the 3-inch mortars was 'Christ, you must have fired these things a lot. There's no rifling left!' Again, shades of Churn, a mortar bomb fell short when we came in on one attack. An officer in the Devon Yeomanry gave us a lecture on gunner/infantry coordination, and the North Irish Horse provided Churchill tanks. Our training with armoured support went well, but later on in action I found out that one elementary point had not been passed on. We were advancing behind our tank across a flat, open area when we came under Spandau and rifle fire. I spotted where it was coming from, but the tank commander probably did not hear it over the noise of his engine, as there was no return fire from his turret. I spent a highly frustrating time hunting around for a telephone to give him a target indication, but could not find where it was. It was no good thumping on the armour, so as he continued to lumber forward we closed in tight on the blind side.

One of our training night attacks was spectacular. Tracer bullets from the supporting Brens from D Troop set fire to some haystacks near the objective. When we got close enough (just under 200 yards) we stopped to let the PIAT (anti-tank weapon) fire three bombs into the building. Then a Verey light from PC brought down covering fire from Peter and Queenie sections as we stormed in, and a new item of equipment, the Lifebuoy flame-thrower, set the barn ablaze. We cleared the area before moving on to take up all-round defence positions beyond. Sod's law decreed that McMasters, who was a strong chap, found himself lumbered with the flame-thrower after his expertise with the petrol cooker as volunteer cook. On 27 March we returned to Sector A1, and continued our night patrolling to dominate the southern part of the Tongue.

CHAPTER 7

The Battle at Comacchio

2 Commando Brigade opened up the offensive in the early hours of 2 April 1945; the main Eighth Army push started on 9 April; and in western Italy the American Fifth Army's attack was launched on 15 April. Our aim was to capture the spit of land between Lake Comacchio and the sea from the River Reno to the Valetta canal, a distance of about seven miles. The purpose was to draw German reserves across to the east coast away from the main attack, and to try out new amphibious equipment. The plan was for 2 Commando and 9 Commando to use Fantails, larger Storm boats and smaller Assault boats to land on the inland side of the Spit (the main German defences were along the coastal area). 2 Commando was tasked to capture two bridges across the Bellocchio Canal so as to cut off retreat from the south. 9 Commando were to attack enemy positions in the south-west of the Spit. 43 RM Commando had to clear the tongue of land east of the Reno, cross the river, and take enemy strongpoints in the south-eastern part of the Spit. 40 RM Commando would make a feint attack in the sector of the line along the south bank of the Reno which we in E Troop had previously occupied. One of their Troops supported by tanks would cross the Reno farther west to clear the enemy dugouts along the north bank. When the south of the Spit had been taken, 43 RM Commando would advance north from Bellocchio on the coastal side with 2 Commando alongside on the west by the lagoon.

SBS (Special Boat Service) and COPP (Combined Operations Pilotage Party) patrols did their best to find out the depths and nature of the bottom of the Comacchio lagoon. There had been less snow and rain than average during the winter, so the water level was at least 6 in lower than usual. It was known in advance that the Storm boats would have to be hauled over 500 yards before they could be launched empty, and another 1000 yards before they could take a full load. Each boat weighed three-quarters of a ton – a difficult burden for eighteen men to man-handle across glutinous mud, especially when they had 70 pound personal loads of arms and ammunition. It took another seven men to carry the outboard engines and paddle equipment. Another major problem was an Argine, an artificial staked dyke which would impede 2 Commando in particular. There were two gaps, and some places where it was awash, making it possible for boats to be dragged across. Folboat crews would be stationed at intervals to flash morse code navigation signals to assist boats to steer towards the gaps. One artillery FOO (Forward Observation Officer) team with a 22 set

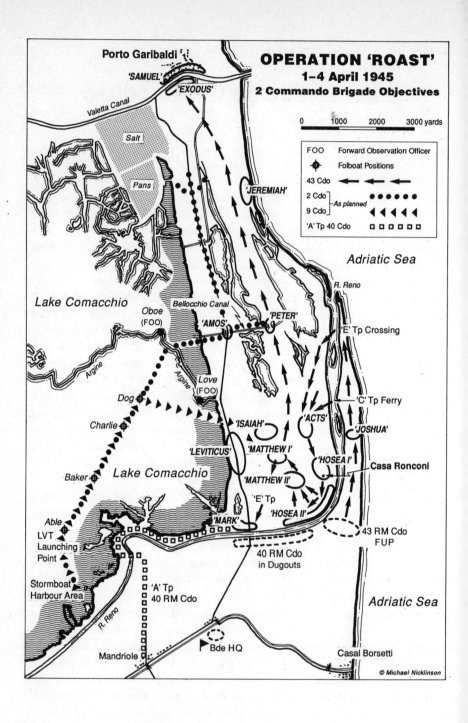

** above:** Large dug-out through the south bank of the Reno in Sector A1. Bob Collins, Jenkins's MOA, is on the far right.

right: E Troop NCOs. Left to right: Sgt George, Cpl Iredale, Cpl Hill; Cpl Jackson seated.

Left: L/Cpl Eddie Webb, seated centre. He made friends with everyone, including this local dog.

Below: Fantails of W Squadron, RASC Fantail Regiment, on the muddy banks of the Reno, 2 April 1945. (IWM NA.23641)

Above: Commandos wearing para-
smocks moving up past Churchill
tanks fitted with their deep wading
exhaust trunking, 2 April 1945. (IWM
BA.23638)

Right: Marines Farrel and Davis, 43
RM Commando, setting the sights of
3-in mortar in the FUP area at the
mouth of the 'Tongue', 2 April 1945.
(IWM NA.23574)

Above: Vickers MMG Section, 2 Commando, Comacchio, 2 April 1945.
Below: Men of 40 RM Commando moving forward over open ground. There was little cover on the 'Spit', particularly on the flat flood plain in the south. (IWM NA.23966)

Above: German prisoners at Comacchio wearing the Einheitsfeldmutze field cap design made famous by the Afrika Korps and the poor quality tunic, the Feldbluse Modell, both introduced from 1943. (IWM NA.23644)

Below: Men of 43 RM Commando skylined while advancing from Bastia to Argenta along the top of the embankment of the Reno, 16 April 1945. (IWM NA.24249)

Above: Stretcher bearers and mortar men of 43 RM Commando being ferried across the Reno near Argenta, 17 April 1945. Note the lower terrace and the bare top of the central embankment. (IWM NA.24252)

Below: Bringing back German and British wounded, Argenta, 17 April 1945. (IWM NA.24257)

...e Mauser bullet (above) stopped
...r the pack.
...agged for life' (below).

...ubaltern who survived.

Above: Humber LRCs of 56 Recce of 78 Division, 18 April 1945. After breaking through the Argenta Gap 6 Armoured Division advanced rapidly northward to the River Po. (IWM NA.24311)

Below: 43 RM officers, just before disbandment, August 1945. Back Row: left to right: Lt J. F. Britz, Lt J. Morris, Capt R. W. Bazeley RAMC, Lt D. C. Leatherbarrow, Capt G. Frost, Capt J. P. Stevens, Lt R. Liddell, Lt M. A. McConville, Lt I. A. G. Webster. Middle row, left to right: Capt M. L. Preston MC, Capt M. R. Nunns MC, Capt R. B. Loudoun, Maj J. C. D Hudspith MC, Lt Col N. G. Munro MBE, Rev R. S. Hook MC RNVR, Capt D. L. Roberts, Capt B. I. S. Gourlay MC, Capt R. N. Parkinson-Cumine MC. Front row: left to right: Lt G. Hawarth, Lt W. G. Jenkins DSO, Lt G. Hazell.

would be on the Argine opposite the Bellocchio Canal, and a second team would be positioned opposite the landing area for 9 Commando farther south. There were still 800 yards to go beyond the dyke, and navigation would be difficult as there was little horizon on the low-lying Spit. Moreover the outboard engines had no neutral, so once started, the boats had to keep moving. Finally none of the craft were likely to get closer than 200–300 yards from the shore, so the last part would have to be waded. It was hoped that the landings and our Tongue attack would coincide at 2359 hrs 1 April.

Considerable work was put in at Brigade and Commando HQs to produce orders and get equipment and supplies to the correct places and properly camouflaged. A detailed programme of supporting fire from 150 guns on request was worked out, and white phosphorus shells would indicate when barrages were about to be lifted. During daylight hours medium bombers and Spitfires would give air support. Once bridgeheads were established, sappers would operate rafts across the Reno and erect a Folding Boat Equipment Bridge. Other detachments would lift mines. On the signals side there were all the code-names to identify objectives quickly. To cover the preparations the artillery gave harassing fire, and 40 RM Commando started to blare out propaganda and Wagner over a loudspeaker.

Two sub-paragraphs in the orders turned out to be prophetic:

5. **Loading of craft**
   It must be appreciated that boat crews will be inexperienced and navigational hazards considerable so that COs must plan and train for landing in the wrong order at the wrong place and with only a portion of the unit.

16. **Timings**
    In view of the uncertainties of approach all timings will be regarded as approx.

For our straightforward task 43 RM Commando was allotted four Fantails, 5 Assault boats, 4 collapsible rubber intruder dinghies, a Troop of Kangaroos manned by 4th Queens Own Hussars, two Troops of Churchills manned by the North Irish Horse, and a Platoon of 42 Field Company RE. Conventional procedures going back to 1914–18 were followed. Parties had gone out at night to lift mines and tape safe routes in front of our line along the south of the Tongue. Neil Munro had laid out white tape to each Troop FUP (Forming Up Position) in the woods behind the line. We all knew what we had to do, as we had rehearsed on similar terrain. After dark on the night of 1 April we moved silently forward loaded with ammunition and grenades, and lay along our tape. Everyone was keyed up and ready to go. The lessons learned from all those countless battle-drills and training attacks were about to be put to the test. When bullets and shells start to fly war is a completely arbitrary affair.

There was the heightened awareness that the next few days were going to be dangerous, but with the optimism of youth I never seriously considered getting hit.

Slowly the time moved on to H hour. No sound of artillery bombardment. Midnight came. No order to advance. We waited ... and waited ... and waited. When one is geared to go there is nothing worse than a delay, and this was particularly the case for A and B Troops. They had to attack the German positions on the Tongue ('Joshua'), so under cover of darkness they had advanced over 1000 yards forward to lie up closer to the enemy. First light was at 0515 hrs, and they would have to get back to our lines before then. Word began to come through that 2 and 9 Commandos were having great difficulty in crossing the lake.

The Brigade Major's report gives the details on what happened. It was two hours behind schedule that the Folboat markers got into position and the Commandos reached the launching area. After prolonged efforts every Fantail got bogged down, and the LVT Squadron Commander reported that it was impossible for them to proceed. 2 Commando had thirteen, and 9 Commando seven, so all those troops had to be transferred to spare Storm boats and Assault boats. Everyone became inextricably mixed. It was well past midnight, so landings by night were now out of the question. Ronnie Tod was at the launching area and could see the confusion. A second attempt would be likely to encounter the same difficulties, and the Storm and Assault boats were afloat, even though they were in chaotic order. The two FOOs on the Argine could bring down smoke to cover daylight landings, so he made the brave decision to go ahead. This was shouted from boat to boat. The Storm boats were paddled into groups of four and lashed together; their engines were fitted on and with a roar most of them started. The disorganised armada set off for the morse flashes with Assault boats in tow behind. There was further physical effort and confusion for 2 Commando when they had to drag their boats over the artificial dyke. One subsection whose engine failed to work actually paddled the whole way across the lake. 9 Commando, on the shorter southern route, came under fire at 0447 hrs and called for artillery fire, which shielded them as they slowly struggled through thigh-deep tenacious mud. Their first Troop got ashore at 0530 hrs. They subdued the gun positions at 'Isaiah', but at 'Leviticus' they were held up by accurate mortar and Spandau defensive fire. This is where the most stubborn resistance was encountered. It was shortly before 0700 hrs that the first units (their HQ and Heavy Weapons Troop) of 2 Commando ploughed their way to dry land unobserved. A German officer managed to blow 'Amos' bridge, but 'Peter' bridge was later taken intact.

43 RM Commando got the order to go ahead at 0500 hrs. By this time A and B Troops had started to filter back. The signal came through just in time, and they returned to their original lying-up position, but the movement

brought down enemy artillery and mortar defensive fire. In E Troop we were close to the fusillade of MMG and Bren-gun fire from 40 RM Commando just to our west. They floated dummy assault boats and figures into the Reno, which attracted the enemy's fire on to their sector, but they were well protected in the deep dugouts. Our guns put down a devastating barrage on 'Joshua' before A and B Troops moved forward to clear the positions. The plan was for C Troop in Kangaroos carrying Assault boats and E Troop in Fantails to pass through and carry out the river crossings. The order to advance came, we boarded the Fantails, the ramps went up, and engines came to life. Escorted by a Troop of waterproofed Churchills we rumbled forward. At long last we were getting on with it.

PC and I were able to stand on a platform at the rear to see what was going on. Three-quarters of the way up the Tongue we came across a stationary Kangaroo from which Marines were staggering out as if they were drunk. The vertical extension to the exhaust had been fitted with the outlet facing forward instead of to the rear. Not very bright, and in the event the Kangaroo was not able to wade the river. When we reached A Troop we heard that Stan Barnes, the Gunner subaltern who had recently joined us, had been killed. Our crossing place was right up near the mouth. The driver of our Fantail managed to get his controls locked and we turned a slow circle in the middle of the river. PC was furious, but I saw the funny side. Nevertheless I took a much closer look at the LVT. To achieve buoyancy the frame was very thin, and gave little protection. Fortunately only Spandaus fired at us, and they were a long way off. We replied with bursts from the more powerful .50 calibre Browning MMG. Our driver still was not doing well. Instead of achieving a straight run to tackle the far bank, he finished his circuit at an awkward angle, and got stuck. With our heavy loads we sank thigh-deep into the soft silt, and it was a difficult scramble up the steep bank. None of the Fantails managed to climb out, but later on they ferried A Troop across.

C Troop had a much rougher time at their ferry point just beyond 'Joshua', as enemy guns were ranged on that locality. During the initial attack on 'Joshua' their Troop Commander, 'Shorty' Roberts, when he saw that A and B Troops were held up by enemy wire, had given the order for his Kangaroos, festooned with the frameworks of Assault boats, to move forward and charge through the obstruction. This sudden intrusion of strange armoured vehicles demoralised the Germans, and induced them to surrender. When the Assault boats were off-loaded to get the ferrying started, it was discovered that two of the canvas skins had been holed by shell fragments. The Gunners and our 3-inch mortars put down smoke to cover the work of assembling the three sound boats and inflating the dinghies. Wooden stakes were driven in on the near bank, ropes were paid out from the craft as they were paddled over, and more stakes were fixed on the far bank. C Troop fanned out to secure a beach-head, the ropes were made taut between the stakes, and a faster relay system was established to take B and D Troops across. Inevitably the area became a target for shelling, and of the eight Marines who manned the ferries four were killed and one was severely wounded.

Meanwhile, at our crossing point, the tank commanders decided that the river was too deep for the waterproofed Churchills to wade across safely. Wet and muddy, we were faced with the daunting prospect of having to advance for over 1000 yards across a flood plain which was devoid of cover, without the protection of being in Fantails, and with no close fire support from tanks. The German strongpoints on the higher ground at 'Acts' stood out menacingly ahead, and as we slogged along we were completely exposed. We blessed the Gunners, who put down an awesome curtain of shells on 'Acts' on a scale unknown to us in Yugoslavia. This protection was especially needed when we encountered a drainage ditch right out in the middle. It was just too wide to jump, and once more we sank thigh-deep into slimy mud. The far bank was very slippery, and several Marines were held up as they failed to get a purchase with their boots. D Troop on our left were pushing ahead, and PC had to keep the majority level, so he told me to round up the stragglers. I scouted round urging them to double forward, and then saw that McMasters was still stuck fast. Mindful of Achnacarry, I ran back, pulled as hard as I could, and he struggled out. The full Lifebuoy he was carrying was a pig of a load, and I did my best to steady it as he gamely stumbled into a trot.

The FOO who accompanied us did an excellent job. He held the HE (high explosive) until we got close enough to run in, and then brought down smoke. We swept across their positions, turned, and took them from the rear. At each fortification we called on them to surrender. As we commanded the vulnerable entrances they stood no chance against bombs and bullets. Still dazed from their battering, they filed out with their hands up. The shells which had saved our lives had shattered many of theirs. One man was lying on the ground with the whole of his left shoulder just a pulp of flesh, blood and bits of bone. He was fighting for breath with great gasps. Four men passed me carrying a blood-soaked blanket from whose sagging depths emerged pitiful groans. We had to leave the Germans to do their best for their own wounded. Those unhurt and able to walk we organised into large squads to cut down on Marines needed for escort.

Our next objectives, 'Hosea I and II', were back farther south. The bombardment from the guns and our quick follow-up induced surrender rather than fighting. Many more prisoners were taken. 'Hosea I' was particularly interesting for me as I had to clear the farm buildings of Casa Ronconi, which I had seen silhouetted by fires during my patrol. On the advance towards 'Hosea II' I spotted movement behind the second hedgerow to our front. I got the men down, pointed out the target area to Sergeant Abrams, nominated a

Bren-group and four riflemen, and told him to double forward and engage the enemy while I took the rest of the half-Troop right flanking. We moved fast to the far side of a hedgerow which led in the right direction and gave some screening. I kept up the pace until I reckoned that we were far enough forward to be just behind the enemy. Then we turned left and advanced quickly in extended line across a large field to cover on the far side. As I had hoped, it provided the perfect position from which to assault. About a dozen Germans were in fire positions facing away from us along a hedgerow to our half-left. Their attention was focused on the fire section, so when we burst out they were taken completely by surprise. To give them a chance I called out 'Hände hoch' ('Hands up'), and they quickly laid down their weapons. At the top of my voice I yelled to Sergeant Abrams to cease firing and close up, and we took all of them prisoner. Speed had been the secret of success.

The German officer in charge was a big man, smartly turned out in a well-cut uniform and peaked round cap. He came up to me and said, 'What did I do wrong?' When I looked surprised both by the question and his ability to speak English, he repeated the query, and added, 'How did you know we were here?' I told him that I had seen some movement. He towered over me accusingly and said, 'Why aren't you black?' When I looked even more surprised he again pressed his point. 'We were told that there were black troops opposite us.' This Johnny Prussian obviously took his soldiering seriously, but it was not up to me to sort out deception by his superiors. Looking back, it might have been his usage of 'black' instead of 'foreign' which made the exchange so bizarre – we had relieved the Gurkhas in the line. I reminded him that he was now a prisoner. He had a leather map-case and when I told him that I would have to take it in case it contained useful marked maps, he made no demur. A strange twist of fate was to make this acquisition of the utmost significance, though I had no time to open it up just then.

At 'Hosea II' we cleared the dugouts along the north bank of the Reno. Always we had the upper hand, as we were taking them from the rear. The prisoners required yet another escort, and some men had been wounded, though not seriously, so Troop strength was getting depleted. 43 RM Commando had taken all its planned objectives, and the whole of the south-eastern part of the Spit was under our control. At Troop level we were unaware of the difficulties faced by 9 Commando at 'Leviticus', so it was not good news when the order came through that we had to take 'Matthew' in their sector. Again there was magnificent support from the guns as, similar to 'Acts', we advanced three Troops up in extended line north-westward over the flat flood plain towards well-prepared defences on higher ground. Fortunately they were manned by troops from the Turkoman Division (see Appendix 2) recruited or conscripted in the East after the Germans initially overran most of the Ukraine. They had no desire to lay down their lives for the Reich, and were ready to capitulate when we reached them.

For E Troop there was to be no respite. The Troop from 40 RM Commando had been held up by anti-personnel mines and Spandau fire in trying to clear the north bank of the Reno eastward. One of their supporting tanks, after using fascines to get across ditches, finally got bogged down, and the other Churchill was brought to a halt when its track was blown off by a tellermine. We were ordered to finish clearing the dugouts in their sector 'Mark'. Ours not to reason why, so, while the rest of the Commando moved north to 'Peter' bridge, we set off south for the extreme south-western corner of the Spit. It was late in the afternoon, but we could see the tracks used by the Germans through the minefields, so it was easier for us. Now practised at winkling out the occupants of dugouts, we linked up with A Troop of 40 RM Commando as dusk fell, and asked them to take charge of the prisoners.

A great effort was required to gear ourselves up for the march to 'Peter'. No one had had any sleep the previous night, as we were on the *qui vive* the whole time waiting to go. Since dawn we had been continuously on the move. The distance as the crow flies was just over three and a half miles, but it seemed a never-ending plod in the darkness. A very weary bunch of men rejoined the Commando at about midnight. We were taken to the slit trenches previously dug by 2 Commando, and sentries were posted. The Germans subjected us to intermittent shelling, including some large-calibre 'Casa Crushers', but hunched in the confined holes in the ground we were so tired that we got some valuable sleep.

The next morning, when PC was out recceing, Ian Riches came up and congratulated us all on the way in which we had kept going the previous day. Then he went round to talk to individual Marines. Afterwards he took me aside and said that he had noticed that the men were not shaved, and that it was important for morale to keep up standards. Somewhat indignantly I pointed out that we had not yet had any resupply, so there was no water left in our bottles for us even to have a drink, and as regards morale we would much prefer to push on straight away rather than have to burrow around in our packs to find razors to attempt a dry shave. He did not press his point, and later on jerry cans of water and 24-hour ration packs arrived.

The original start-time had been 1100 hrs, but there were problems over rebridging at 'Amos'. The previous day 2 Commando had encountered heavy fire from strongpoints when they probed northward, so the Brigadier wanted tanks to get across to support them. The delay was most welcome, as it meant that we had time to make a brew and have a much-needed cooked meal. When I opened the map-case I found there was a bonus: a pair of light desert-issue binoculars, and a good camera. We set off at 1400 hrs and before long came across 'S'-mines – the warning signs 'Achtung Minen' ('Beware mines') were still there. This was another anti-personnel device whereby if you trod on the detonator prongs it shot up to chest height and the explosion scattered ball-bearings. With my half-Troop I followed what seemed to be a beaten track, but there was the lurking anxiety that schu-mines might have been sown as well. To the right a couple of rearguard Spandaus covered the route – we heard the fast bursts of fire. When we emerged from our minefield and were able to get across we found that the other group had been caught completely in the open. Marine Maclean had been killed. Sergeant George was seriously wounded, and his face was tense with pain. Corporal Dutton had slit the blood-soaked leg of his battledress all the way up to apply a tourniquet. We stretchered him back to Doc Bazeley straight away. Sergeant McKenna had been shot through the buttocks, but he was so profoundly relieved that the bullet had only grazed another part of his anatomy which was dangerously close that he was quite perky. Another Marine was lightly wounded.

Alick Maclean, at twenty-eight, was older than most of the Troop. Before the war he had gone to Argentina, where he was well-set to become manager of a large sheep ranch, but he was determined to come back to volunteer. All of us respected his steadiness, maturity and Scots grit, and it was a great loss that such a man had to give his life.

Further on we came across an abandoned heavy-gun position, where a line of dead German soldiers lay sprawled close together among the coarse grass of the dunes. Most of them were stripped to the waist, and their mess-tins lay alongside, indicating that they were taken by surprise whilst queueing for their midday meal. The bodies were turning grey-blue, so they had been dead for two or three days. What puzzled me was that several of them had no sign of any wounds at all. An aircraft must have spotted them and dropped a bomb close, so maybe shock-waves did the damage. Whatever it was, they all died suddenly.

The Germans had withdrawn from 'Jeremiah', which we had been tasked to clear. The Valetta canal and Porto Garibaldi were not far off, so when fighter-bombers flew in we had a close-up view of their bombs falling on the town. The orders to the Commando had been to probe the defences along the canal, with a view to 9 Commando exploiting our success farther north. C Troop went through as point troop, and we followed behind. The last 600 yards in front of the canal was flat, and almost devoid of cover. When C Troop had committed themselves out in the open they came under heavy fire. Corporal Tom Hunter, in charge of the Bren-group of the leading section, spotted that some houses near the south bank were occupied. He seized the Bren, charged forward on his own, and ran through the houses firing from the hip. Six Germans surrendered, and the rest retreated across a footbridge over the canal. Having eliminated this danger, he took up an exposed position on the south bank, and engaged the concrete pill-boxes on the other side of the canal with accurate fire to enable the Troop to get forward to the houses he had cleared.

Inevitably the Spandaus focused on him, and he was killed. Corporal Hunter was awarded a posthumous Victoria Cross. He was the only Royal Marine to win this medal during the Second World War, and the citation ends: 'Throughout the operation his magnificent courage, leadership and cheerfulness had been an inspiration to his comrades'.

'Shorty' Roberts had been hit out in the open. Marine Skinner stayed with him, and then managed to get back to our position in the dunes. He was absolutely insistent that we should go to him straight away. It was still daylight, but I took out a stretcher party and hoped that the white flag would be respected when we walked out in full view of the canal. Skinner knew exactly where to go, and when we reached him 'Shorty' was his usual unruffled self. After having been out in the sun for a couple of hours, he was very grateful for a drink of water. When it healed, his arm was not fully flexible, but I heard that later on he ran the Cliff Assault Wing at Sennen, so he did not let the handicap restrict him.

On the first day both officers in B Troop were unlucky. 'Barney' Barnett, the Troop Commander, was wounded by a schu-mine. David Leatherbarrow's injury was unusual. The unfortunate Marine in front of him had his foot blown off, and it flew up so that the heel of the boot caught David's eye. He lost his sight on this side, but was able to have a light artificial eye fitted. (At a reunion dinner some years later he started to fish around in his soup. When I asked him what he was up to his reply was, 'I've lost my eye'. It was tracked down, cleaned and restored. Join 43 to learn the etiquette of eye-handling at table!)

Porto Garibaldi was too strongly fortified to justify an attack, so we held the new line that night and throughout the next day. In the darkness of 4–5 April we were relieved by a battalion of the Coldstream Guards. The standard strength for Infantry Companies was 120 men, whereas out Troops had been reduced to well below fifty. Enemy shelling and mortaring had restricted our daytime movement, so the Guardsmen had to dig many more slit trenches. The march-out was now more than seven miles, and we had the novel experience of crossing the Reno over a bridge. We were delighted to find that transport was waiting to take us all the way back to billets in Ravenna.

The Brigade took 946 prisoners – we accounted for three Infantry battalions, two Troops of Artillery, an Anti-tank unit, and three Companies of heavy Machine-gunners. 43 RM Commando's tally was 450, for the loss of one Officer and eight Other Ranks killed, and three Officers and thirty-eight Other Ranks wounded. The message of congratulation from the Eighth Army Commander, Lieutenant General Sir Richard McCreery, ended, 'All ranks have shown a splendid enterprise, endurance and determination to surmount difficulties. Your success has helped the whole army plan. Well done indeed!'

PC managed to get hold of some transport, and the two of us tracked down our wounded. Sergeant George put a brave face on things, but it was obvious that both he and the medical staff were worried about the condition of his foot. Later we were greatly saddened to hear that gangrene had set in and he had to lose his leg.

After three days we had to go back to relieve the Guards. This time I was right up front in a *casa* in Scaglioca. The young subaltern who briefed me was completely unaware of the need to keep his voice down – we were only 130 yards away from the Valetta canal. I reminded him that he was not in his London club, and that I had no wish to get stonked, so he did tone down his disconcertingly loud delivery. By lying low during the daytime, except for the lookouts, we kept things quiet until we were relieved on the night of 11–12 April by 28 Garibaldi Brigade.

Despite their failure on our operation LVTs were used successfully to lift two battalions of 167th Infantry Brigade across flooded land for a right hook on Menate, which helped to outflank Bastia to the north. In this operation 40 RM Commando had to capture a pumping station and bridge on the south-western shore of Lake Comacchio. Eventually they were successful, but they got caught in a very exposed position in daylight, and it cost them a quarter of their strength in killed and wounded.

After the 43 RM Commando 50th Reunion in April 1995 the CO of Comacchio Group, Lieutenant Colonel Robert Wilsey RM (whose father was a Troop Commander in 46 RM Commando when I joined them in the latter part of 1945) travelled to Italy with eight members of his unit. Using photo-copies of my wartime 1/25,000 maps Mike McConville gave them an account of Operation 'Roast' on the ground. The Tongue is now a restricted military area where Air Defence weapons are tested, but the British Embassy in Rome arranged clearance for them to visit it. The party discovered that the pine wood at our FUP has been cleared, but the dramatic change is that coastal erosion has foreshortened the Tongue by over 3000 metres. E Troop's crossing point up by the former river mouth has passed into oblivion, and today the northern tip is about 400 metres south of C Troop's ferry point. The two stone buildings of Casa Ronconi on the western side of the Reno are still there.

Just south of the Valetta canal a memorial stone has been erected to Caporale Inglese Thomas Hunter VC, Caduto per la Liberazione d'Italia, alongside commemoration of four Italian Partisans who were also killed near Porto Garibaldi in April 1945.

CHAPTER 8

Breakthrough at Argenta

On 15 April we moved up to Conselice, which had recently been captured. The next day we marched north towards Bastia, with sections staggered in single file on either side of the main road. Everything was on the move – lorries, guns, tanks, jeeps, carriers: we were part of an advancing army. Suddenly we turned off left down the embankment to a flat flood plain. After all the noise and activity and the feeling of being part of a whole, the stillness of the quiet countryside was unreal. We moved across to relieve the Buffs along the bank of the River Sillaro. There was nothing but flooded land to the north, and not a sign of the enemy. The next day we moved round to the dyke bordering the Quaderna canal. Still only a few enemy stragglers. We seemed to be in limbo on the banks above a waterlogged terrain.

Four dykes border two canals and the River Reno immediately west of Argenta, and they run parallel close together north-westward for three and a half miles before the Reno bends west. Each is about thirty yards wide, with a high central flat-topped embankment about ten yards wide. All the land to the west had been flooded by the Germans. Tactically this area was a menace, as there was no cover and not the slightest room for manoeuvre. Well dug-in positions across the dykes had a complete advantage. An extract from the *Official History* reads as follows: 'To help 78th Division, 2nd Commando Brigade (less 9 Commando) was given the ambitious task of fighting its way alone along the western bank of the Reno, under Fifth Corps' command, to outflank Argenta.'

Early on the morning of 17 April, 2 Commando, helped by accurate preliminary bombing from the air, launched successive assaults on narrow fronts to capture the three bridges crossing the two canals and the Reno just west of Argenta. Over the next five hours units of 42 Jaeger Division put in four counter-attacks. They were all broken up by Bren-gun and small-arms fire, together with effective artillery support. Over twenty of the enemy were killed, and many were wounded. Our E Troop position was just south-west of the Reno, close to Bastia on the other side. We became aware that the limbo was not to last when groups of extremely frightened Italian peasants came running south along the embankment. I remember one pretty young girl in particular, bare-legged and bare-footed, wearing only a short, thin grey shift which outlined her figure. Her face was puckered in distress, and she kept looking back; she must have lived in the houses near the bridges.

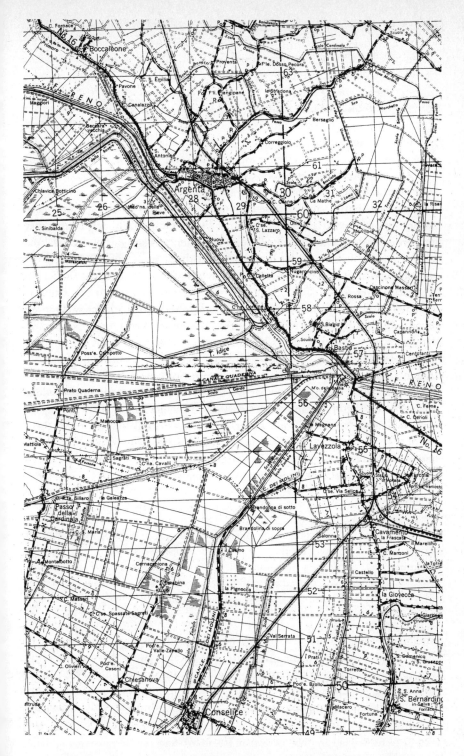

WAR-TIME 1/50,000 MAP OF THE ARGENTA AREA

The task for 43 RM Commando was to clear the banks up to the bend in the Reno a mile north-west of Argenta on the night of 17–18 April, in conjunction with a strong attack by 78 Division to the east of the town. 40 RM Commando took over our positions, and we moved forward in daylight to a FUP just behind 2 Commando. A and B Troops were to clear the Reno and central canal embankments. D and E Troops had to advance along the bank farthest west to capture a pumping station, and some houses beyond it. C Troop, depleted after Comacchio, supplemented A and B Troops. Churchills from 48 Royal Tank Regiment were to assist us.

An extraordinary last-minute development enables me to give a more accurate account of the battle. I was aware that PC had a sister, though I never met her. Royal Marine contacts helped me to trace her, and she was pleased to hear that I would be dedicating this book to her brother. Cecily very kindly gave me a photograph of Ralph, and then sent me a long letter which I had written to PC shortly after the Argenta action. It was a strange sensation to be reminded of what happened by one's former self. I remember that the letter was rattled off rapidly, and it reveals my immaturity. A censor physically cut out some gratuitous swear-words before PC's belongings were sent home from Italy! Nevertheless it conveys the 'fog of war', so extracts are well worth quoting.

At 0330 hrs 18 April there was an inauspicious start. The leading tank, badly damaged by a mine, slewed across the flat approach section, and made it impossible for the other tanks to get past on to the embankments. Once again we were deprived of close fire support. On the restricted lower terraces there was no alternative but to advance in irregularly spaced file, which spread the men out. I had forgotten that we in E Troop originally set off along the eastern terrace and D Troop were to the west. The letter makes this clear:

Dear PC,   4 May 1945
I was very relieved to hear that the Bishop [nickname for Padre Ross Hook – prophetic as it turned out, as he did indeed become a bishop] found you all right, and that he gave you the gear you requested. I've been waiting to get your address. Well, here's the whole story. It'll be a long screed, so I hope you survive!
You remember you shoved off with Roger [Section] and HQ from the bridge? I got a very indeterminate message to follow on, and having collected Cpl Joshua and Lawson, who didn't know whether you'd gone or not, I kicked off too. We went quite a way, until I began to wonder whether I'd made another balls-up and gone off too soon. I was relieved to see Woodger [PC's Marine Officer Attendant: batman and runner] when he came back to find out where we were. We continued behind him until the 4.2 [4.2-inch larger calibre mortar supporting us] fell short, and Joe [Woodger] got it in the arm and hand. I was nearest, and put down my Tommy gun to get my field dressing out. Kent [Marine trained in First Aid] turned up pretty soon and took over, but there was such a crush there by that time that I couldn't find my Tommy in the dark.

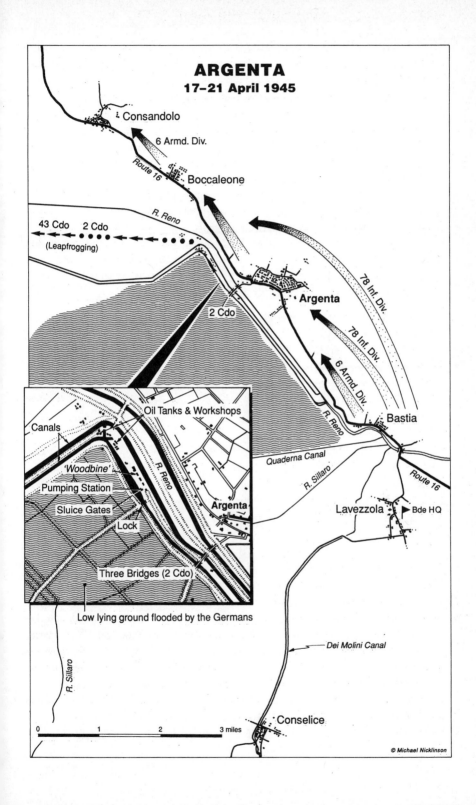

ARGENTA
17–21 April 1945

Consandolo

6 Armd. Div.

Route 16

Boccaleone

R. Reno

43 Cdo   2 Cdo
(Leapfrogging)

2 Cdo

78 Inf. Div.

Argenta

78 Inf. Div.

6 Armd. Div.

Bastia

R. Reno

Quaderna Canal

R. Sillaro

Route 16

Lavezzola   ▶ Bde HQ

Inset map

Canals

Oil Tanks & Workshops

R. Reno

'Woodbine'

Pumping Station

Sluice Gates

Argenta

Lock

Three Bridges (2 Cdo)

Low lying ground flooded by the Germans

Dei Molini Canal

R. Sillaro

Conselice

0   1   2   3 miles

© Michael Nicklinson

Then you suddenly appeared, and told me to take Peter [Section] on to clear the buildings. When I peered over the central embankment I saw a vague shape forward to the left (west) so we crossed over. As I was advancing along the western terrace I was challenged by a pussers [naval slang for 'correctly done'] 'Halt, Ver Dar?' ['Who goes there?'] from about 30 yards in front. Then the blighter opened fire. This wasn't according to the rules of the game *à la* Comacchio at all [many Germans had readily given themselves up], so I turned round and called up the Bren-group, having first of all tried my 'Hände Hoch', which didn't work. Same old trouble again – there was no damn Bren-group anywhere near. The only chaps there were Cpl Iredale about ten yards behind me, and Murkett, Landon and Youngman keeping very quiet about ten yards behind that. I borrowed Cpl Iredale's Tommy and started giving the Jerries a few bursts whilst I got nearer. I was so close that I was able to locate them easily – two riflemen dug in on a bank behind an iron-barred fence, and a Spandau position with three men, dug in on the flank of the central embankment. There was another Spandau drilling away on your side of the embankment.

The next sequence of events is still etched vividly on my mind. The Spandau was firing over my head, and I realised that he was unable to depress enough to get at me. The fall of shot was much further down the embankment, where men in the long file were huddled against the bare central bank. If I gave the Germans a burst to keep their heads down I could scramble up on to the central embankment and, if there was no position on top, I might be able to find a route round the fence to outflank them. It would be easier to use Mills bombs from there.

Fear made my stomach sink deep as I launched myself up the bank, as it was impossible to avoid becoming hopelessly skylined. Six yards in front were two 12 ft-high ornamented iron-barred gates set between brick pillars. They were a couple of feet ajar, which made me deeply suspicious. No one fired at me, so I advanced cautiously and felt carefully for any trip-wires attached to a booby-trap. Finding nothing, I edged my way through, stopped and listened. Nothing to be heard. Slowly I walked forward ten paces, stopped and listened again. Not a sound. I realised that I must have passed behind their positions. There was nothing to be gained from going further. I turned and made my way back to get support. When I was abreast of the edge of the gate, the stillness was broken and things happened fast.

Just below the crest to my left (east) there was a muzzle flash. Red sparks flashed in front of my eyes, and I felt a searing pain in my neck. As I swung round there was another shot. A kick like a mule in my back lifted me off my feet and I was flung face down on the ground. Dazed by the impact, my first thought was that I had been mortally wounded, and that shock had deadened pain. Religion has never been my strong suit, so I wondered whether I would be on my way up, or whether I was booked for down below. Letter again: 'I found that old Mephisto didn't seem to be hollering for me.' It occurred to me that I was still thinking pragmatically, so I tried moving my arms and legs. They worked. Still lying flat, I unclipped my pouch, took out a Mills bomb, released the lever, held it for a couple of seconds because they were so close, and lobbed it very gently over the edge. I didn't score a bull's-eye on their unseen trench, and it must have exploded just in front. The Germans were not keen on this sort of retaliation. There was a sudden swish as someone legged it fast down the embankment and along the bottom terrace. Complete silence for another minute. Then another swish as a second man made a run for it. This time I followed him with a burst from my Tommy gun, but I am sure I didn't hit him, as it was dark below. Silence again.

The letter adds an incident I had forgotten:

> I still thought I heard movement in their dugout, so I came closer to the edge and bunged in a 77 (phosphorus smoke grenade). There was no one there, and all it did was to set off the Spandau ammo.

The next sound was a faint rustle, coming from below ground. Quickly I hit the deck, and started feeling around with my hand. I found that I had been knocked flat close to a slit trench. There had been a position on the top after all! I took my Colt .45 out of its holster, cocked it, put my hand in the hole and fired towards the front. Something shot up under my nose like a jack-in-the-box. In the dim light a man was dancing in front of me with his arms up, gabbling out, 'Don't shoot! Don't shoot! I'm Austrian. I'm Austrian' in a terrified voice. Fortunately for me he had not been a brave soldier, and had crouched in the back of his slit trench throughout. I stood up and told him that I would take him prisoner. Not long afterwards I spotted something white being waved just below the edge of the embankment to the right. The three men from the western Spandau position, no doubt aware that I knew where they were, and not wishing to be a target for further Mills bomb practice, had decided to give themselves up when they heard me take their comrade prisoner. The Austrian was unlikely to make a run for it, so I moved across and stood over their dugout. They emerged cautiously, eyeing the muzzle of my Tommy gun with distrust, and put their hands up smartly. They were followed by the two riflemen from the slit trench a bit further away. At long last Corporal Iredale appeared on the top – the only man who had dared to move.

We were taking the prisoners back when PC suddenly appeared from over the embankment, and slithered down. He seemed to be having difficulty in breathing, and I suddenly realised that he had been wounded. After quickly taking off his equipment, I saw that he had been hit in the chest, so I immediately sent Iredale off to get a stretcher and carrying party. I investigated as best I could, and found that the dark-bluish holes were not bleeding too badly. He was a very strong and determined man, but even he knew that he couldn't go on. It later transpired that his right lung had been punctured. When the stretcher arrived he adamantly refused to take it. Thinking that he was doing the stiff upper lip bit, I pressed him very hard to change his mind. It was lucky that his wiser instinct prevailed, as the surgeon told him afterwards that staying upright prevented his lung from flooding, and probably saved his life.

Back to the letter:

> You were mighty stubborn not taking the stretcher, but there you are, it may have been easier for you walking. I've kept your smock – its got a luvly bloody 'ole in it. I've also got a little souvenir for you – the metal shoulder that got shot off your 36 [Mills high explosive grenade]. When I looked in your pouch the pin was damn nearly out!! Some of the rounds in the bandolier you were carrying in your right pouch went off – did you feel 'em?!!

So PC used up three of his nine lives in one go, and I was pretty lucky that the pair with the Mauser rifles missed me from seven feet!

Probably as a result of PC going back, two messages filtered forward to me. One was that John Page, the Gunner Captain commanding D Troop, had been wounded in the leg and foot, and the other was that Lance Corporal Webb had been killed. Eddie was a delightfully cheerful and friendly man who got on well with everyone in the Troop. One felt that he should not have had to go into action, as he bore not the slightest ill-will towards anyone, and violence is the last thing that he would have been associated with. The news meant that I was the only officer left, as Joffre Britz, John's subaltern, had had to go into hospital a few days beforehand. I rounded up Queenie Section, and took them forward to clear the pumping station.

> We'd just got through the gates and were negotiating some wire when I spotted a German officer with a Schmeiser leading a single file of riflemen out from behind the buildings. He stopped in complete surprise. My reactions were much faster than his. I dashed over and stuck my Tommy gun in his ribs. His men, as surprised as he was, made no effort to offer any resistance. The officer turned out to be a major, and he was most indignant when I pointed to his watch and binoculars for him to hand them over. Though he protested volubly in German I reckon that it's fair game to acquire them on the battlefield. We took the nine prisoners back, and I rounded up the men from Dog Troop. They'd had trouble such as we had during the afternoon – apparently someone told half of them to go back. Anyway, the other half were there, so I took them forward, and we cleared the first houses opposite the pumping station without finding anyone.

By this time I had tied up with the E Troop signaller, so I reported back to Commando HQ, and told them what had happened. Neil Munro ordered me to consolidate where we were, and not to advance further to 'Woodbine'. For some reason I was hanging around on my own on the central embankment north of the gates. It had lightened considerably, so visibility was no longer a problem. Suddenly I spotted another file of Germans coming out from behind the building. There was not a stitch of cover, so all I could do was to crouch down. The seven of them stopped and started chatting to each other. Their rifles were slung over their shoulders – they were in no hurry to move to the slit trenches. It looked as if they were waiting for some more to catch up. They obviously had no idea that their comrades had been attacked during the night. I had to hold on in case any of the stragglers might run back to raise the alarm.

I waited tensely. No one looked in my direction. Two men did appear, and joined the group. Still I waited, to make sure that they were the last. Then I stood up, marched forward, and bellowed out 'Hände hoch!' They just stared at me, dumbfounded. I advanced to a few feet away, swung my Tommy gun along the whole bunch, and rapped out the order once again. Still they did not react. The dreadful thought crossed my mind that I might have to mow them all down. Then at long last their leader began to unsling his weapon, and handed it over. The rest obediently followed suit, and laid their rifles on the ground in response to my gestures. I motioned them away from their weapons towards the gates. In the light of my experience with the Spandau team I kept a sharp watch for any movement towards grenades. Once again the reliable Corporal Iredale turned up just at the right moment with my MOA and some other Marines, so the prisoners could be searched properly. The leader, the equivalent of a Sergeant Major, handed over his watch to me without a word. Later, when I had time to examine my pocket, I discovered that it was a slim Swiss jewelled-action model which has been my faithful companion all over the world for the last fifty years. The Major's watch was a cheap affair which I gave to my MOA, Rob Collins.

There were still more surprises to come. Immediately north of the iron fence there was a line of tall poplars, and beyond them the slope of an offshoot leading from the central embankment west to the pumping station. Fully forty minutes after the capture of the morning relief, white handkerchiefs were waved above ground on this bank. Four more Germans gave themselves up. Although it had been light for some time, we had failed to spot these slit trenches. It brought home to me very strongly the importance of clearing the objective. Anyway, now it really was clear, so I allocated fields of fire to the sections, and they dug in.

Neil Munro came up on the wireless and told me to get the lock gates opened just to my south-west. This was to enable people to get forward in Storm boats, to which I gave scant credence. However, I did what I was told, and was very surprised to find that at this early hour there was an Italian on the other side. After shouted attempts at Italian and a great deal of gesticulation, I managed to persuade him to open the gates. Highly delighted with this achievement, I reported it back. Needless to say, nothing came of the amphibious plan, and carrying out the order just made the flooding worse.

Suddenly a tall figure appeared opposite us on the parallel embankment east of the canal. He was beating his arms and stamping his legs in the chill of the morning. The likelihood is that he had come with the morning relief, as he was unaware of our presence. A Bren-gunner from D Troop, whom I did not know, eagerly asked if he could shoot him. Neil Munro had told me that a group from B Troop had not yet returned from the operation, and I was genuinely concerned not to make a ghastly mistake, so I gave this as an excuse. In his long greatcoat there was no doubt at all that he was a German. The truth of the matter was that I was unwilling to kill a man in what I considered to be cold blood. My humanitarian feelings proved to be costly, as he turned out to be a real professional.

Ten minutes later Spandau bullets rattled the poplars above my head. The German had spotted us. The Bren-gunner looked down at me again, and this time got my immediate permission to go ahead. The straight edge of the top of the embankment was a dangerous fire position, so the Marine was careful to come slowly into the aim. He was just about to squeeze his trigger when the German beat him to it. He gave a gasp, clutched his shoulder and slid down into my arms. Two bullets had gone through, but fortunately they were clean wounds with no bones hit. Similarly to PC, they were bluish and not bleeding much, but I got hold of a field dressing from a Marine in case they bled after the initial shock wore off. The Bren-gunner was able to walk unaided back to the First Aid Post, which eased my conscience a bit. It was as well that we were dug in, as the Germans must have cottoned on to the fact that we had established ourselves near the pumping station.

We got well dug in before the stonk came down – pretty heavy stuff, about 150 [mm] I should think. There was also a Spandau just opposite us on the embankment to the east. The bloke was damn good, and drilled a D Troop Bren gunner through the shoulder. We got laced up by 25 pounders [maybe our intelligence wasn't too good, either] as well as the 150s at one stage, and were very lucky not to have any casualties. When the shelling eased off the Spandau continued to fire bursts half way up the trunks of a line of poplars. I was standing at their base, well below the line of fire, and couldn't believe it when a muffled voice called out 'I've been hit' from the bank in front of me. A ricco [ricochet] must have caught him – that's what Herman was aiming to do. Cpl Iredale, after all his sterling efforts [he was awarded a Mention in Dispatches], was the man hit. By keeping our heads down we were able to get him on to a stretcher, as the slit trench was just below the crest line.

During a chat with Walter Iredale at our recent fiftieth reunion I discovered that a fixed memory and, in this case, even an account written shortly afterwards, can be slightly inaccurate. Walter agreed that the Spandau gunner had been aiming for ricochets, and he reminded me of the flurry of leaves which fluttered down after each burst. However, he had not been *in* the trench, as I had assumed from the muffled voice. During a lull in the shelling he and Youngman had begun to dig a new slit trench. His shoulder must have come just above the crest line, and he reckons that it was a full-blooded bullet that smacked into him, probably fired by a sniper. The embankment opposite us was only about fifty yards away, and his upper arm and the joint were shattered. No disability is noticeable, but he is not able to raise his left arm above the horizontal. Initially he did not feel much pain, and I remember how calm he was throughout the evacuation.

At about 11 o'clock Neil came up on the wireless, and said that we had to withdraw. I argued very strongly indeed against this, and pointed out that if the Germans reoccupied their positions it would be extremely difficult to dislodge them a second time. Moreover, the Spandau opposite us made evacuation dangerous. Neil said that I had to obey orders, as they came from Brigade. Letter again:

> I organised a fire plan to try to subdue the Spandau – 2-inch mortar, PIAT, and the Brens. He just joined in more, even through the mortar smoke, and the blighter got close enough to knock the mud into my face when I was spotting for the mortars. In the event he only hit a D Troop man – through his steel helmet. Luckily there was just a superficial wound on the top of his head. I bet he'll swing the lamp [naval slang for telling a heightened story] about that in the years to come! We went right back almost to that first house we occupied before the attack, and had a wash down, grub cooked for us, and a good rest.

Doc Bazeley had a look at my neck. Small iron splinters from the gate had embedded themselves, and he got most of them out. (The couple that remain have never given any trouble.) The other bullet entered the bottom left-hand corner of my large pack, smashed its way through the recently acquired camera, passed through the rolled hold-all containing my toilet gear, penetrated the mess-tins, and ended up in the biscuits in my 24-hour pack. Two of the small teeth splayed apart on the brass section of my razor-head give a daily reminder of another kind of close shave. It was ironic that my best bit of loot, albeit gained unwittingly, should have helped to save my life.

A and B Troops had been heavily engaged from the east bank of the Reno early on in their advance. Mike McConville was wounded. When the enemy attacked they were held off with Brens and rifles, and 2 Commando were able to assist with overhead supporting fire from their 3-inch mortars and Vickers machine-guns. The Germans suffered severely on the open terrain, and later on evacuated their casualties under a white flag. Mark Nunns, B Troop Commander, had pushed on to his objective 1000 yards north of the start-line, but only had one section left with him, as the rest of his Troop had been pinned down by the counter-attack. On the way back in daylight they encountered the enemy, but with a quick charge he and his men seized the initiative. They took an officer and four men prisoner. Mark was hit in the leg – his third wound received in action: all in the same leg. Years later in Malaya he was wounded for a fourth time. Guess where!

Orders came through from Brigade that we had to repeat the attack again that night, 18–19 April. The left (west) flank of Argenta had to be cleared right up to the bend in the Reno so that 6th Armoured Division could advance safely up Route 16. After Comacchio and the attack the previous night we were five Troop Commanders and three subalterns short. As I knew the ground, I was put in command of an amalgamation of D and E Troops, and was given a Wasp [a flame-thrower mounted on a tracked Bren-gun carrier] in support. It was pleasing to be given the responsibility just after my twentieth birthday, but if the fence was defended we would have trouble, as the only possible gap was through the gates. We set off at 0100 hrs, and I kept the Wasp at my shoulder close behind the point section, as its spurts of flaming liquid would be vital to subdue the enemy and cover our charge up on to the central embankment. All of us were tense as we silently but steadily advanced. Quote again:

> We came across Joe Woodger's pack – he was hit further back than the rest of you. Then we found Beale's body about 40 yards in front of the Spandau position – he must have been leading. I'd no idea that he'd been killed. Did you know at the time that he'd been killed? Several people from B Troop had asked me about a body they'd seen on our side when they were withdrawing down the central embankment, but no one had told me anything about it. I knew that Beale was not with his section, but thought that he must have been one of the wounded to go back. The gunner hit five of you – Lawson, Upton, and Wolstenholme as well as yourself.

There was no firing this time. I halted the point section well short of the gates, crawled forward and listened. Keeping as low as possible I edged on to the central embankment. The gates were still open as they had been the night before. Very conscious of the slit trench on the top, I wriggled my way through, and found that the positions were unoccupied. I breathed a tremendous sigh of relief and went back to bring the Troop on.

My next concern was whether the Wasp could get up the steep slope, but it managed it, and got through the gates and round to the pumping station. Our task was to clear a group of houses code-named 'Woodbine' about 500 yards further on. We came across two German officers and a couple of soldiers who gave themselves up. When the first building came in sight I gave the point section a final briefing on the drills for house clearance (the course at Battersea did come in useful!). After an anxious wait the Marines came back with broad grins on their faces. I soon found out why. The farm had been a brothel (reason for the morning relief not knowing about the night attack?), and the camp followers were still in residence in their flimsy night attire. The women eyed us with considerable interest, but they were a dirty, slovenly lot, and I shepherded the Marines out smartly, as I could see that they would not have minded if our progress had been delayed for half an hour. As the other buildings proved to be empty, our morale rose sharply. It really seemed certain that the Germans had withdrawn completely.

Some hefty bombs must have been dropped on 'Woodbine', as there was a large crater in the middle of the road through the houses. In the dim light I was walking two feet in front of the Wasp with my arm jabbing left to steer it round. The confounded driver ignored my signs, and persisted in veering to the right. I bellowed at him at the top of my voice, but to my disbelief he continued to the rim of the crater, the carrier teetered, toppled and overturned to the bottom. There were muffled cries for help which became woozier, and I had to shout at the idiot again to turn off his ignition to avoid carbon monoxide fumes and the danger of fire. Flammable liquid was spilling out, and the whole crater reeked with the smell. The Marines responded really well, and set to with their spades with great energy, but it was a hell of a job to dig a hole big enough to be able to prise open an exit. I suppose the driver had very limited vision in the dark, but I did not have much sympathy for the crew when we dragged them out in some distress, gasping for breath. My men had saved their lives.

After this annoyance and unnecessary delay I shook the Troop out into formation again. Once more armoured support had been more of a hindrance than a help. We continued our advance, and the letter has reminded me of the last leg, which I had forgotten about.

> The arty [artillery] barrage had been much better laid on this time, and on the broader northern section had set some oil tanks alight. It was like the Western Front just beyond 'Woodbine' – oil blazing away everywhere, smashed trucks in light railway sidings, and wrecked workshops.

Thankfully nothing was occupied, and we reached our objective (the northern bend in the Reno) without further incident. It was most satisfying to report that the western embankment was completely clear. The other Troops also met no opposition along the central embankment and the banks of the Reno. We dug in, but did not get much rest, as next morning 2 Commando came up and took over our position, and we were ordered to advance another 1000 yards westward across the unflooded flat land which opened out between the Reno and the two canals. Instead of being restricted to file we moved forward in a wide extended line. We picked up two more officers and twenty-six other ranks, but all of them gave themselves up without offering any resistance.

> The chaps kept going well although they were bloody tired. Once again we dug in, and got some sleep in the afternoon. That evening Neil informed me on

the wireless that 6th Armoured Division had driven through the Argenta Gap and was fanning out to the north of us. I passed the message on to the men. That night Charlie [Troop: reorganised, like D and E] and ourselves – the old firm base [can't remember the significance of this] – and 2 Commando went about four or five miles further west, and we dug in next to Joe Nicol, Jerry Jermyn and 5 Troop [2 Commando]. We actually stayed there for the rest of the night.

Next day when we continued the advance and reached the main road leading from Molinella up to Ferrara, whole columns of Germans were moving south. One paymaster sergeant major spotted that I was an officer and with his methodical German training asked me for a signature to relieve him of his responsibility for his unit pay. In the horse-drawn wagon beside him were thousands of negotiable Italian lire which he would have handed over if I had written 'John Smith, Lt' on his official form. I could not do it, and told him to hand over the money further back. I just hope that some base-wallah dealt with it properly, and that it wasn't appropriated.

The good news that we were being pulled out came on 21 April, and the whole Commando assembled at 'Woodbine'. Ronnie Tod congratulated us on our success, but drew attention to the fact that officer casualties had been high, and warned us to be more careful. We did not get the chance, as on 2 May 1945 General von Vietinghoff, commanding Army Group C, accepted unconditional surrender and a ceasefire throughout his area of responsibility in northern Italy and southern Austria.

Lieutenant General McCreery sent a final message to Ronnie Tod: 'Now that final victory has been achieved I want to send you and all ranks of your brigade my very best congratulations on your splendid share in the battle. After your successful SPIT operation your troops showed a magnificent fighting spirit combined with skill and enterprise in difficult operations which enabled V Corps to break out of the Argenta defile. This success was the decisive phase of the whole battle. Well done indeed.'

I see that I vented my feelings to PC on the difficulty of getting support at the sharp end. There were signs that I was growing up a little more.

> You probably know that we've reorganised into three Troops now, and Easy has been kept intact. When we formed the new Troop I had a pow-wow with the Senior NCOs first, and then the Juniors. I told them that in handling their sub-units they must use their own initiative more to get their men forward so as to exploit any advantage gained in initial contact.
>
> When we first reorganised I was in charge faute de mieux, so young Clueless [PC's nickname for me when I was slow on the uptake] had to keep really switched on – far too energetic a performance!! Ian (Gourlay) didn't go on that course, but went into hospital instead. He returned and took over the Troop three days ago, so I'm back in good hands! Joffre Britz has come out of hospital

earlier than expected too, so there are two of us as subalterns. If he holds the fort
Ian and I may be able to get down to see you. We've just heard the good news
that things are officially over in Italy'.

I visited the General Hospital at Forli as soon as I could after the battle.
Unfortunately PC had been sent all the way down to Bari, but I managed to
see Corporal Iredale, Lawson, Woodger and Upton (wounded for the third
time). PC had left pencilled notes to say what he required. As usual, everything
was itemised down to the last detail:

Beret with badge – 1 (old beret, well polished badge)
Razor, Razor blades (he left nothing to chance with me!)
The numbers of his Paybook and Identity Card (issued in Plymouth September
1940)

Significantly, two books – *History of Modern Europe* and *Anthology of Modern
Verse*. He was a much better read and rounded man than his undergraduate
subaltern. I found what he wanted, and Ross Hook took his things down.
Final extract from the letter:

By the way, what do you want doing with your kit – you've got an awful lot
of gash [naval slang for spare stuff]. It was a great pity that we missed each
other, but there you are. As regards the wounded Sgt McKenna [from
Comacchio] has just gone to a Con [Convalescent] Depot from 11th General.
I don't know which one. His chopper was only grazed, and his buttocks are
healing well. Woodger, Upton and Lawson are all in 5th British General. Jack
Bolton managed to see them there today. I'd heard that Joe [Woodger] could
lose the use of his hand, but apparently it's going to be all right now, thank God.
Upton is starting to walk again, and Lawson is having a bit of skin grafted on
somewhere. Mark Nunns was also there, and should be pretty fit soon. Cpl
Iredale is in the 93rd at Barletta – Cpl Jackson heard from him today. He is pro-
gressing well, but is having bags of penicillin shoved into him. Sgt George
[Comacchio] is still cheerful. He kept on being mistaken for an Itae [see Troop
photograph. Dark-haired, he is sitting next to me] – I read one of his letters. He
is in the 22nd at Taranto, waiting to be invalided home I believe. Miles and
Skilbeck are both in a Con Depot somewhere. Wolstenholme, by the way, was
very lucky. He was another of those bullet-through-the battle-bowler boys, but
he too only had a superficial wound on the top of his head. He was waiting for
us in Ravenna when we got back.

How are you getting on now? Everyone has been asking about you, and they
all send their regards. Moreover the nurse at Forli said that you were 'a fine boy'
when I asked her how you were!!! Better not tell that to the lady love from
Totnes. I found her photo instead of your identity card to begin with. A
far more satisfactory substitute!! Give my regards to Mike [McConville] and

Leathers [Leatherbarrow]. I hear that his sound eye is working overtime looking lecherously at all the nurses.

Get well soon.

Yours Aye,

Jenks.

Ian and I did not manage to get down to Bari before PC was invalided home. He made a good recovery – later on he was posted as an instructor to Achnacarry! After 43 was disbanded I had returned to Oxford before I saw him again. As I had lectures to attend I left a note in my rooms telling him when I would be back if he arrived when I was out, ending it 'in statu pupillari'. He added a footnote which fixed a definite time for us to meet. It was signed 'Soldatus'. No flies on those CS men!

CHAPTER 9

Interlude in the Far East

At long last (our batch had been Johnny-come-latelies) the men could look forward to seeing their families again in the not too distant future, but in the meantime there was little improvement in their day-to-day lives. We spent some time guarding prisoners in hastily erected barbed wire compounds at Bellaria, on the coast just north of Rimini. On one occasion I and three Marines escorted a column of several hundred Germans down to the beach to give them a swim. This cheered them up, and on the way down and back they combined wonderfully in their singing, which I much enjoyed.

I was delighted to receive a pass for a week's leave in Florence. The Town Major gave me a room in the Hotel Savoia with Lieutenant Morgan, an older subaltern from 2 Commando. Martin Preston was there too, but as he was now a Captain he had his own room. This break came at a most opportune time for me. During the six days in the Argenta area we did not get much sleep, and hard-tack food had been snatched irregularly. Close encounters with Spandaus are not all that relaxing, and we covered some distance beyond the bend in the Reno. As at Deal, the body registered a complaint, and raised a small red volcano on my side, which became very painful. In the hotel I was able to apply hot poultices, and the massive boil burst. Fortunately it cleared up, and I did not have to report sick.

It was marvellous to have seven days to enjoy the pleasures of urban civilisation in the knowledge that the fighting was over. We savoured our food and wine to the strains of a string orchestra, and every night a pretty Italian singer lulled us with a soft rendering of 'Hear my song, Violetta'. Martin was genuinely attracted by her charm, and did his best to get to know her, but she courteously held him off. I went to a performance of *La Traviata* at the Teatro Comunale. Violetta was sung by Bruna Fabrini, Tullio Serafin was the conductor, and it was produced by Hans Busch. Slow on the uptake as usual, it was a long time before I realised that the popular song was based on the opera. The theme from Verdi's overture became firmly implanted in my subconscious, and often wells up when I am in a relaxed mood.

VE (Victory in Europe) Day came a week after the surrender in Italy, but it was not a time of celebration for me, as I was sorting out the affairs of the three Marines who had been killed. Personal effects were pitifully limited. Subscriptions were organised, and their close friends were most generous, but money helps little. I explained where they were buried, and tried to express the contribution that they had made to our life in the Troop. Thankfully I must have hit the right note, as I received replies from all three families, which impressed me with their dignity. (In Eddie Webb's case it was from his brother-in-law, who said that Eddie's young wife was too overwrought to write, which did not surprise me. Only at the recent reunion did I learn that she had had twin daughters.)

I had a stroke of luck, through Marine Hyatt. He had been sent on an Advanced Cookery course (at this late stage!) and I was given permission to proceed on duty to Udine to pick him up. A jeep and driver were provided; we were to be given accommodation as required, and I got the Adjutant to route us via Venice on the way back. At Udine we found that the course had moved on to Klagenfurt, so my 'swan' (free trip) was further extended. The drive over the Alps and along the Worther See in southern Austria was most scenic. Carinthia was where Hitler had his 'holiday camps' – blond, blue-eyed Party members were sent to produce Aryan babies for the Reich. When I spent the night at the Officers' Club it was amusing to find that the cabaret was exactly the same as in Ravenna, the only difference being that the Austrian girls were more heavily built than their Italian counterparts. On the way south across the dull Po plain I offered to give the driver a relief, and unwisely he consented. I knew that a Scottish regiment was due to Beat the Retreat in St Mark's Square and I flew along far too fast to be in time to watch it. The unfortunate driver was in greater danger than he had been in action. At one point there was a slow-moving Italian cart with wooden sides slanting outwards, and in whipping round it I just caught the windscreen frame and cracked the glass in front of the driver. Nevertheless I continued the headlong rush and reached Venice in time. After the Retreat I took a gondola, and as we glided towards the Rialto Bridge a huge yellow moon hung low in the dusky sky. A romantic setting, but sadly there was no fair companion to share it.

I already had a reputation, dating back to my days on Vis, when I had swept in to park a jeep and had impaled it on a pole sticking out from the rear of another vehicle, having been unsighted after driving up a steep incline too quickly. Windscreens were almost irreplaceable on the island, and I shall never forget the look of horror and incredulity on the face of the Transport Sergeant who happened to be right on the spot. This time the CO decided to put on some pressure, and ordered an official Board of Inquiry. Bob Loudoun, who was Adjutant at the time, dropped heavy hints about the dire punishment that could be inflicted, but failed to intimidate me. The day came; I was marched in, there was formal questioning, but I got away with a reprimand, and was not fined.

Ian Riches (who later became Commandant General) did not hold these escapades against me, as he invited me to become a Regular. This was an honour, and the offer was tempting, as I thoroughly enjoyed soldiering.

Nevertheless I felt that after the heightened wartime experiences, peacetime routine might become a bit repetitive and restricted. I decided to return to Oxford so as to become a teacher, feeling it would be more rewarding to help youngsters to contribute to a wide variety of occupations.

At the beginning of June the Commando moved to a tented camp outside Naples prior to our return home. I managed to fit in a visit to Pompeii. Vesuvius had erupted fairly recently, so pervasive dark grey volcanic dust still lingered everywhere. Nothing to compare with the cataclysmic explosion in 79AD when the whole city was buried beneath layers of cinders, small volcanic stones and ash to a depth of 22 feet. The inhabitants were asphyxiated by poisonous gases and the fine dust. The excavated houses and wall paintings, the mosaics, the shops and the columned temples, and the chariot grooves and stepping stones in the streets conveyed a lively impression of what life in a Roman town was like. In addition there were the numerous artifacts on view in the museum as well as the poignant plaster casts made of some of the victims.

*   *   *

To digress briefly, I had close contact with active volcanoes after the war. In the summer of 1949 two Yale friends and myself stayed with a most interesting man, Gustav Regler, in the village of Tepotzlan in Mexico. During the 1930s he had been an influential underground Communist in Germany, and he took part in the civil war in Spain as a political commissar. He told me that he well remembered the activities of Josip Broz (Tito).

Paracutin had recently erupted, so we went to see it. To reach this remote spot we approached on horseback by night through a First World War land-scape of black ravines and ridges. The piteous arms of bare trees were sil-houetted in the moonlight: a blanket of hot ash had destroyed the vegetation for miles around. We came in sight of a line of twinkling lights, which next day we found were caused by the crust crumbling away from the edge of the lava flow to expose red-hot surfaces. At irregular intervals fiery 'bombs' were hurled into the night sky. As the horizon slowly lightened, the cone with its plume of smoke became visible, already 500 feet high above former flat maize fields. A remarkable feature was that the tongue of acid lava swung left only 50 yards short of a small Catholic church. The priests must have made much of that! When we went down I chose my moment to scramble up the steep edge of the flow, though there was one surge of heat from a collapse. On the flat top it was safe, as there was a rough scoriaceous surface, like clinker.

In 1968 I took a party of Brathay and African boys to survey the crater of L'Engai volcano (9480 ft), twelve miles south of Lake Natron in Tanzania, after its spectacular eruption two years earlier. Soft unconsolidated ash on the lower slopes and a steep, slippery crust higher up made it a *tour de force* to get the equipment to the top. Instead of the former deep bowl which had 800-foot terraced cliffs on the southern flank there were now two shallow basins separated by a central ash ridge curving down from the eastern rim and up to the western crest-line. I climbed down to the lip of the open vent – there was still constant rumbling and churning going on down below.

*   *   *

On 19 June 1945 we embarked at Naples on the *Caernarvon Castle* and sailed back free from submarines and air attack. As we came up the Solent I remember how green the countryside looked after the parched landscapes in Italy. My mother must have given a huge sigh of relief when I appeared on the doorstep, though there was still Japan to be reckoned with. Several officers went down with malaria or jaundice, and a couple with both, but I escaped.

We reassembled after disembarkation leave at Oakridge Camp near Basingstoke in Hampshire, but 43 RM Commando was disbanded, and we were gradually dispersed. My posting was to 46 RM Commando, which was stationed in civvy billets in Tonbridge. Bill Bailey, my Troop Commander, was a large, jovial HO officer, easy to get along with. Mike Hincks had campaigned with 46 across north-west Europe, so I met up with him again.

On 2 September 1945 a Japanese delegation formally signed unconditional surrender documents on board the *Missouri* after the Emperor had intervened to say that the unacceptable admission of defeat was necessary in order to avoid mass destruction. The prospect of fighting in the Malayan jungle had not appealed to me in the least, so this was great news. It meant that 46 RM Commando no longer had an operational role, and it too was run down.

In the autumn of 1945 the Chiefs of Staff decided that the Royal Marines would be responsible for the Commando role in peacetime, so the Army Commandos were disbanded. This must have caused some heartache, as Army volunteers had been the first to undertake offensive raiding operations in the dark days of 1940. (Brigadier Peter Young DSO MC gives a stirring account of their activities in his book *Storm from the Sea*.) At that time the Royal Marines Division had been fully committed to home defence, as the threat of invasion was very real.

As a result of this decision 45 RM Commando embarked on the escort carrier HMS *Rajah* in January 1946 to replace 1 and 5 Commandos in Hong Kong. I was in charge of a draft of forty-four Marines, thus enabling men from 42 RM Commando to return home after their close-fought battles at Myebon and Kangaw in the Burma jungle. Ian Gourlay, Bob Loudoun, Mike McConville and Nick Demuth were all in 45, so we had a pleasant voyage, with plenty of deck hockey.

When we entered harbour, the whole draft, which included a Wren detachment, lined up on either side of the flight deck to pay compliments to other ships. At Colombo a seagull perched on the flagpole at the stern, and remained there for some time with a used condom in its beak, which must have embarrassed the girls.

Admiral Mountbatten came aboard, and instead of inspecting us he walked straight up on to the bridge and told us to break ranks and gather informally below him. He spoke straightforwardly to the Marines, and his delivery was charismatic. One joke referred to a visit that he had made to Bali. The authorities were concerned about the way in which the women dressed traditionally, so as he drove by they all lifted up their grass skirts to cover their breasts.

42 RM Commando was stationed at Stanley Barracks on the Taitam peninsula at the southern tip of Hong Kong island. One of our jobs was to try to control the looting on the Peak, just behind Victoria. Most of the former rich residences were still empty, and the Chinese stripped them of everything. The Marines had to repeat the double warning 'Ting ting', 'Ting ting' before opening fire, by which time the looters had escaped, so I was thankful not to be involved in any inquiries. There were some expert Chinese thieves – one Marine had his watch removed from his wrist while he was sleeping at night. In the overcrowded tenements of Victoria and Kowloon the necessities for life were in short supply just after the war, and it was not unusual to come across gaunt dead bodies lying in the back streets.

A few days after my twenty-first birthday the CO, Peter Hellings (who also later became Commandant General), told me that I could put up a third pip, as he was giving me command of W Troop. We were sent on detached duty to the small coastal village of Sai Kung, about nine miles east of Kowloon on the mainland. A couple of interpreters helped me in my dealings with Mr Lee, the head man, and I was able to assist over such matters as rice supplies, medical help and the problem of finding a schoolmaster to teach the children. I had seven Japanese prisoners of war under my command to help with the community work, which further widened my experience of other nationalities. With fair treatment they were most willing and effective workers.

Many people in the rural areas were animists, so I found out which trees and stones had sacred associations – I did not want the Marines unwittingly to cause offence. The Chinese pay great respect to their ancestors, and spend their limited money on paper replicas of things which their former relatives might need, and on firecrackers to ward off evil spirits.

My other task was to carry out anti-pirate patrols, for which I was given an old naval launch. I rigged up some rough and ready water skiing by paying out a wooden plank from the stern. By standing on one end and heaving up the other with my hands I got some fun. We boarded and searched numerous junks, but failed to find much. An intriguing incident was the discovery of a Communist hospital on one of the islands. The staff seemed unconcerned about concealing their identity, as the nurses wore the familiar red scarves. This was the interim period when Chiang Kai-shek and his Kuomintang Nationalist

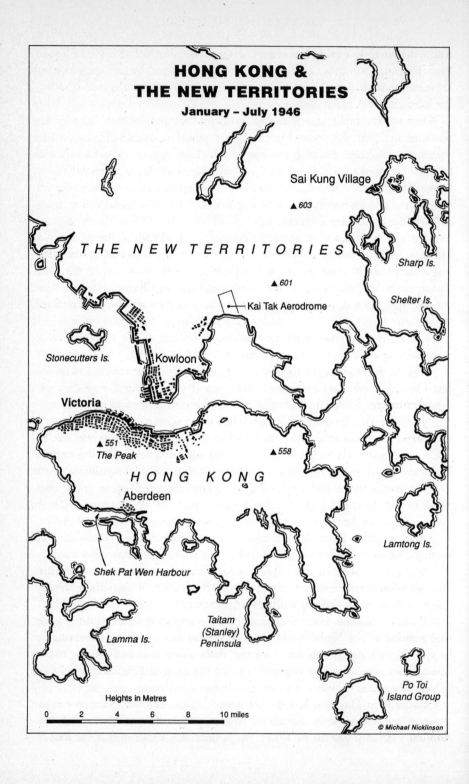

HONG KONG &
THE NEW TERRITORIES
January – July 1946

Sai Kung Village

▲ 603

THE NEW TERRITORIES

Sharp Is.

▲ 601

Kai Tak Aerodrome

Shelter Is.

Stonecutters Is.

Kowloon

Victoria

▲ 551
The Peak

▲ 558

HONG KONG

Aberdeen

Lamtong Is.

Shek Pat Wen Harbour

Lamma Is.

Taitam
(Stanley)
Peninsula

Po Toi
Island Group

Heights in Metres

0   2   4   6   8   10 miles

© Michael Nicklinson

regime had been re-established in government after their isolation in Szechwan. Mao Tse-tung's fortunes had been dramatically improved by his acquisition of Japanese weapons and equipment in the north, as had been the case with the Partisans after the Italian surrender.

When we returned to Hong Kong island I encouraged the men to get qualifications and sent the promising ones on promotion courses. Firing on the ranges was maintained; there were guard duties on strategic installations and the War Crimes Court; I ran discussions on current affairs; and sports fixtures figured large. At the end of May drill took precedence in preparation for an inspection by Brigadier 'Jumbo' Leicester RM (whom I was later to meet again in Washington DC while I was at Yale).

I managed to visit the small Portuguese colony of Macau on the western tip of the broad bay leading towards Canton. The buildings around the harbour had a distinctly Mediterranean aspect. Gambling was the main activity, but that interested me not at all. I came across the British Embassy and decided to call in. The Consul much appreciated a chat, as he had been isolated all through the war.

Release from the Navy was much quicker than from the Army so in July I embarked on another escort carrier, HMS *Atheling*, for the return trip back to England. In preparation for civilian life I bought some white shirts and shorts and a pair of black leather shoes at cheap Service prices from the naval 'slops' (Quartermasters' Stores) on Blakangmati Island just south of Singapore.

My service with the Royal Marines lasted three years to the day. With normal Class A release I received my full gratuity and all the leave that was due to me, so although I left on 9 August I was paid my 32s a day until 13 October. For demob clothing all ranks were treated the same, and I chose the standard issue double-breasted grey pin-stripe suit. The cloth was quite good, and although the cut was not Saville Row it did me perfectly well for many years. I dined in a pukka Mess for the first and only time on my last night, where the Regulars wore Mess Dress. I had been astonished when PC once hauled his out from the bottom of his tin trunk on Vis, so at least I knew that they existed. I didn't mention that I'd put an additional ribbon up, as I was awarded the Distinguished Service Order after the Argenta action, which pleased the family.

I had been one of the lucky ones. Of the other five from OCTU who went into the Commandos, Peter Collins and Brian Lindrea were killed during the reoccupation of the Netherlands; Donald Murray lost a leg, but subsequently became British Ambassador in Sweden; Peter Dietz switched to the Army Education Corps after the war, and reached the rank of Brigadier; and Mike Hincks completed his medical training to become a GP.

Captain John Day and Ralph Parkinson-Cumine did their best to get an Independent Commando Parachute Troop established in 1948, but the Admiralty decided against it. When the Korean war broke out at the end of

COMBINED OPERATIONS HEADQUARTERS,

1A, RICHMOND TERRACE,

WHITEHALL, S.W.1

27th August, 1945.

Telephone:
WHitehall 9777

Dear Jenkins,

I am delighted to
see that you have been awarded
the D.S.O.   Please accept my
sincere congratulations.

Yours sincerely,

R.Laycock.

P.S.   There are not many
Subalterns walking around
with D.S.Os.
Well done.

Lieutenant W.G. Jenkins, DSO, RM.
No. 43 (RM) Commando,
C.M.F.

Congratulations from Major General Laycock on the
author's decoration

ght: The start of the Circuit to test
e senses – touch, hearing, smell
d taste.

low: For river crossings each
oup had to improvise a raft from
oden planks, barrels and lashing
e. If they used their initiative their
rvival bags could increase
oyancy.

While some rafts were successful, others were not. A cold lesson in winter. A penalty was imposed if the time limit was not met.

The two-mile stretcher race carrying a casualty.

For aerial ropeways groups were provided with scaffolding bars, swivel clamps, heavy ropes, strong iron stakes, a ledgehammer and a spanner. They had been taught how to tension ropes. Over rivers only one crossing in a one-man canoe was allowed. It paid to think of hauling packs across on karabiners to make individual crossings easier.

Rock climbing on the cliffs at Baggy Point, near Croyde, North Devon.

Helming a 55-ft Army yacht.

L'Engai eruption.
Top: The southern 800-ft terraces, August 1960.
Above: Ash-filled southern basin, August 1968. The arrows indicate the same rock bastion.
Left: The central ash ridge, 1968.

above: The 400-ft northern cliffs, 1960.
below: Smoothed northern slopes and open vent, 1968.

Expedition to Everest Base Camp, 9 April – 16 May 1983
Above: Yaks were load carriers above Khumjung (12,100 ft)

Below: Everest, 29,028 ft (just visible with its snow summit, centre background) from Kala Pattar, 18,720 ft Nuptse, 25,850 ft, is on the right.

June 1950, Ralph was an instructor at the RM Officers' School at Stonehouse Barracks in Plymouth. The Second-in-Command of the School, Lieutenant Colonel Douglas Drysdale, began to form 41 (Independent) RM Commando, and invited Ralph to join him. Cecily sent me a booklet which gave a short history of the unit in Korea. In the bitter temperatures of late November 1950 the Royal Marines pushed north from Hungnam to reinforce American Marines at the Chosin Reservoir. Between Koto-Ri and Hagaru the Chinese Communist Forces closed in and split the column, setting several vehicles on fire. Under heavy mortar and small arms fire, PC went across to help one of these, and was not seen again. For four years his parents and Cecily endured the agonising uncertainty that he was 'Missing'. It was not until mid-1954 that the seventeen surviving Royal Marine prisoners of war were repatriated. As there was still no factual information Ralph was posted as 'Presumed Killed in Action'.

CHAPTER 10

Leadership Training
at Sandhurst

After another two years completing my degree at Oxford, and a year studying at Yale University on a Henry Fellowship, I joined the staff of Christ's Hospital School at Horsham. As in the Marines, I was fortunate to be teamed with a wise and experienced Senior Housemaster, Arthur Rider, who also commanded the school's Combined Cadet Force. I took a commission as a Sub-Lieutenant to make sure that I would get back into the Marines in the event of another conflict. During Corps training I passed on lessons that I had learned during the war, and acquired the nickname 'Keeno'. 'Housie' was a rewarding place in which to teach, as numerous endowments enable it to offer a boarding school education to boys from widely different backgrounds. They are all provided with the distinctive Tudor dress of long dark blue frock coat with silver buttons down the front and white neck-bands overlapping at the throat, dark breeches with buttons at the knee, and yellow stockings. There is a strong community spirit, a good academic record, and no snobbishness.

Half-way through my six years at CH I took advantage of an opportunity to teach for a year at Hilton College, Natal. There I found that drill was the only form of Corps training. Half the contingent had completely unserviceable rifles which must have dated back to the Boer War, and the Juniors only had wooden cut-outs. The Headmaster gave me permission to introduce fieldcraft, patrolling, map-reading and platoon attack battle-drills. I had to instruct the cadet under-officers and cadet NCOs beforehand but the changes began to work and the boys took to fieldcraft in particular. In addition I tracked down a UDF (Union Defence Force) unit in Pietermaritzburg and arranged for a regular senior NCO to bring up rifles and Brens from their armoury once a week to give the Seniors instruction in weapon training.

In 1956 I took up an appointment at the Royal Military Academy, Sandhurst and we moved to Camberley. My official appointment was initially as a Senior Lecturer in International Affairs, and then in Communication Skills, but after my spell in the Services I got on well with both the senior officers and the captains. As a result they accepted my offer to take part voluntarily in exercises in the field. To begin with I helped on weekend exercises on Dartmoor and in North Wales. After that, when work permitted, I obtained permission from the Director of Studies to go on overseas exercises, as I was prepared to live out in the field with the cadets and Directing Staff for the whole time. They asked for my views during debriefs, and sought my opinions on the leadership qualities of cadets. As a former Other Rank, albeit only for a short time, I was able to give an assessment from two different perspectives. My time in the ranks also enabled me to get on very well with the NCO instructors, for whom I had the highest regard.

Counter-revolutionary warfare had been added to the conventional training. This involved concealed all-round defence at night, and the setting up of road-blocks and cordon-and-search operations by day. Directing Staff (DS) officers who had been involved in the Malayan, Cyprus and Kenya Emergencies set high standards. Since the 1970s the cadets have been given realistic initiation into handling civil disorder in built-up areas. For example, WRAC Other Rank girls dressed in civilian clothes role-played irate Irish housewives, and harassed the cadets with strong verbal abuse. Amidst swirling black smoke from burning tyres the cadets had to protect themselves from a variety of missiles, including real petrol bombs. Some of us from the Communication Department would appear at hectic incidents with a microphone, subjecting the cadet in charge to aggressive interviewing to try to provoke him into unguarded replies. This was filmed with hand-held cameras, and quite a few cadets were embarrassed when the tapes were played back, but they learned from their mistakes.

In the early 1960s we flew to the former huge American Wheelus Airbase outside Tripoli. The training area was on the *hammada* (stony desert) just south of Jabal Nefusa, which is dissected by former river valleys which are now dry except for occasional flash-floods. In Roman times the climate along the North African coastal area was much wetter than it is today. The terrain was a real test of map-reading as with so few features the cadets had to interpret the contouring. One cadet in charge on a night exercise insisted on sticking to his compass bearing which took us over a difficult broken ridge. He could easily have worked out two bearings and have paced distances along flatter ground to make a detour. For once justice was done as it was he who sprained an ankle. To save the whole platoon being held up, I offered to stay with him, and the DS Captain arranged for a recce vehicle to pick us up. Left with the radio, I had to use wartime 'Able' 'Baker' 'Charlie' signals procedure instead of the NATO code. The cavalry officer was terse in dealing with this jargon, but I helped him to get to the right spot.

When I first went to Cyprus in December 1962 there were strong Army garrisons in the Sovereign Base areas at Episkopi and Dhekelia, and Akrotiri was the largest overseas RAF base. We were able to use the Kyrenia range, whose southern flank rises abruptly from the central Messoria plain. I have a vivid memory of Hunter fighters zooming up under our noses when we were dug in along the sharp crest-line. I returned to Cyprus a dozen times – doubtless attracted by the warm climate. On one occasion I was in the back of a 3-tonner with a platoon of Gurkhas and their eyes almost popped out of their heads at the sight of so many goats, as it was close to their Deshira festival. Their OC bought (legitimately) a goat which they slaughtered for their feast, and they kindly invited me along. The Gurkha Demonstration Company at the Academy acts as enemy on exercises and my regard for them remains high, especially now that I have been to Nepal.

On platoon attacks the cadets tended to rush through the objectives, intent on setting up all-round defence beyond. In the debriefs I cited the late surrender of the four Germans at the Argenta pumping station, and advised them to search the positions more carefully. I was not impressed by the way in which they loosed off indiscriminate unaimed fire during assaults. Infantry rifles are now capable of automatic fire and they blazed off long bursts of blanks. I drew their attention to the fact that live ammunition weighs a good deal more than blank (memories of the Solta operation), and that even though they are now more mechanised, resupply does not appear out of thin air in time to deal with a quick counter-attack. On one occasion I was in a good position to observe a night patrol, and could not believe my eyes and ears. The cadets were chatting to each other in normal voices as they crashed through the woods, and the leader was using a torch! I hasten to add that this was an exception, but my comments were caustic as to their chance of survival.

On four occasions I went to the Eifel region of West Germany just north of the Mosel. Preliminary organisation took place in the massively constructed Vogelsang barracks. With true Teutonic thoroughness, half the steep hillside had been excavated and built out as a large level sports ground overlooking a scenic wooded river valley. Aryan statues still remained in health and strength postures, though the swastikas had been obliterated. There was a swimming bath, a fine gym and a bowling alley. On one exercise we had two nights of heavy rain during the counter-revolutionary phase, and as we were in pine forests the trees continued to drip throughout the third night. If the 'terrorists' bumped us we had to move. One cadet platoon commander was not good at evading their attentions, and after our third move in the wet and dark we all prayed that he would improve. In the thicker mixed forest the noise of wild boars crashing around added spice to night patrols.

The massive pill-boxes of the Siegfried Line had been blown in, but the rows of concrete anti-tank teeth still snaked across the countryside. Cemeteries bore witness to the heavy losses on both sides during the late Ardennes offensive. In 1974 the DS Captain with whom I was working was Mark Phillips, Princess Anne's first husband, and the Company Commander was in the Life Guards. The landlord in one of the inns spoke English and asked if we knew Mark, as he had heard that he was with us. For a laugh the Guardsman Colour Sergeant pretended to be him, but before we left Mark identified himself, which made the landlord's day.

In the mid-1970s there was a high failure rate at the RCB (Regular Commissions Board). Candidates who just failed to reach the standard were advised to apply again in a year's time, but few did, so something more positive was required. Before D-Day Lord Rowallan, at that time a Lieutenant Colonel in the Royal Scots Fusiliers, had been directed to set up a course in Scotland to improve the 'Not Yets' so that they could pass on to Officer Cadet Training Units. Rowallan's aim was to encourage them to think for themselves, and to develop self-reliance and resilience. His philosophy was 'Develop character first and military leadership will follow'. One of the appreciations that he received from a former candidate was 'Thanks for a terrible time'.

With this model to draw on, Rowallan Company was set up in January 1977 to build up the capabilities of candidates who just failed RCB so that they could tackle the Standard Military Course (SMC). From the outset I became closely involved. Officers and Senior NCOs do three-year tours at the Academy, and each Rowallan Company Commander (a Major) makes his own contribution to the course. An excellent team spirit has existed between officers and NCOs, so the cadets gain much from leadership by example. I was able to provide continuity, and to pass on the training methods which had worked well.

A slogan posted in the Lines sets the tone: 'If you haven't succeeded, ask yourself why.' An important feature is that they occupy barrack rooms where, like soldiers, they experience the problems or mutual support which arise from living together. Cadets on the SMC have their own rooms. During the first few weeks fitness is improved through PT, endurance runs, the obstacle course, log-work and swimming. It is essential for a leader to be physically fit, and he must have the extra reserves to urge his men on when the going gets tough. Even more important is mental stamina – the ability to make sensible decisions under stress. Here again a fit man is better able to think clearly.

Formal military training is not duplicated, but they are taught the basics on map-reading, first-aid, the Country Code and bivouacking, and learn how to construct stretchers, aerial ropeways and rafts. An interesting circuit has been devised to test all their senses. Blindfolded, they have to use touch to make their way round obstacles and steer clear of burning hexamine tablets. They are asked to sniff and identify bottles of petrol, paraffin and coca cola, and their taste is tested with a swig of rum. They are expected to hear and identify a thunderflash exploding in water as well as the soft murmur of a girl, wearing perfume, who stands close by. Still blindfolded, they then launch themselves on a death-slide across a lake (having previously been down it sighted) and trust the DS to tell them when to lower their legs into the water to arrest themselves. Finally they have to write a report on the sequence of events.

It is left to them to decide what kit to take for a five-day exercise on Salisbury Plain. First they have to follow up clues to find the 24-hour packs and equipment which have been cached around the Academy grounds. A 20-mile march along the Ridgeway begins at midnight. In addition to their personal packs each section has to carry an awkward 40-pound burden to bring home, so they have to cooperate as a group. Reasonable timings, adjusted according to the weather, are set between each checkpoint. Success is rewarded by some packs being taken forward; failure results in an extra burden or an additional leg. On an individual night-orienteering exercise those who get round quickest get most sleep. As tiredness begins to tell, they spend two days tackling command tasks such as hauling a loaded trailer out of a ditch, rescuing a victim from a mined house, and making river crossings. The key principle is that they must learn at first hand from their own success or failure in the *doing*. The DS stand back and observe and do not step in unless there is likely to be an emergency. During the debriefs, in which the cadets are made to bring out most of the points, attention is drawn to what a leader should 'be' (the quality approach) as well as to what he should 'do' (the functional). It requires good judgement to leave the right amount of pressure on each particular individual to enable him to realise what he can actually achieve. The fourth day is more enjoyable, as they learn the drills for getting on and off helicopters, including rope descents. In the evening they write an account of what they have learned from the exercise, and at dawn on the fifth day all sections compete in a two-mile stretcher race carrying a casualty.

On this exercise each platoon is divided into stronger, middle and weaker sections. There are points both for and against this as a leadership training technique. The stronger sections gain in confidence, as they are generally (but not invariably) better able to succeed in the tasks. The middle groups often improve considerably, as when they cannot lean on the strong men they often out-perform them through their own endeavours. The problems arise with the weaker sections. They tend to get most burdens and least sleep, and lack of success lowers morale. The counter-argument is that a man has more chance to show any leadership potential if he is not competing against stronger members. Moreover, they are being tested, and the DS have to eliminate the young men who are not suited to be in command of soldiers. In certain individual cases cross-posting is useful – the shock of being transferred from a strong to a weak section can make a man try hard to redeem himself.

This exercise weeds out the weaker men, as they are allowed to give up at any stage. Assessment by the DS is very thorough, as every time that a cadet is in command a pro-forma is filled in which records his ability at planning, briefing and controlling, and any good or bad leadership qualities. Command tasks involve small groups, so the cadets are in charge much more often than is the case with platoon attacks. After a Review Board with the Commandant some cadets are discharged, some are cross-posted so that they have to establish themselves in the other platoon, and some are warned by the Company

Commander that they need to improve in particular respects.

Over one weekend all the cadets assist at homes looking after mentally or physically handicapped patients, which makes them aware of the difficulties that people less fortunate than themselves have to cope with. They also get first-hand experience of the pressures placed upon caring staff.

I suggested trying out initiative exercises which we had used during our Commando training. Over an 18-hour period, suddenly sprung on them, the cadets have to find out specific details at five map references (different for each cadet) within about seven miles of the Academy. How they get hold of the information is up to them – they do not necessarily have to go there. Assignments that test them more and gain more points might include, among many others, locating and bringing back a snakeskin, or providing a note from a member on House of Lords paper, a signed script of the day's BBC news or the authenticated fingerprints of the Duty Desk Sergeant at New Scotland Yard. Their accounts of their adventures show that they are stimulated by these unusual tasks, and surprised when they achieve them. Cadets who are not too successful often draw humour at their own expense – an indication that they too have benefited. Again within a time limit, they have to get as far as possible without any money. Credit is given for ingenuity as well as for distance. One cadet did very well to fix free flights to Malta and back, but we had to exclude this particular initiative to save airlines from being pestered too much.

When they are introduced to the basic skills and safety requirements of four Adventure Training activities – sailing, canoeing, caving and climbing – the cadets are treated in an encouraging and friendly way. I admired the skipper of a 55 ft Army yacht for taking on an untrained crew for a boat that size, but he even got all of us to the top of the mainmast in a bosun's chair! On surf canoeing I spent half my time underwater, but it was great fun when one did ride a wave properly. It fell to me to introduce the cadets to caving in the Mendips. Hopefully some Rowallan men may have followed up these pursuits, and have given their soldiers the chance to try them. In illustrated talks on my Brathay expeditions I pointed out where my leadership had been successful, and where I had made mistakes.

The second main hurdle comes in the ninth week. This time the groups are smaller, there is more individual responsibility, and the exercise takes place on the Brecon Beacons or on Dartmoor. Sections are of mixed ability, in the hope that the stronger men will learn to help those who find things more difficult, and that the latter will profit from such leadership examples by their peers. The brief is that they are infiltrating with supplies for Freedom Fighters, so they have to contact agents who give them coded messages. One of the RVs is the top of Pen y Fan, so I have been there many times. Once the cloud was right down and there was a howling gale and we had to hug the ground and dig our fingers in to progress. When we got back to base camp we heard that a member of 21 SAS had fallen to his death over the eastern precipice close to the summit. Rations are deliberately jumbled in a sandbag with deficiencies in some luxury items so that they learn to share fairly. On one day they are given a live rabbit to kill and cook. I had forgotten about Army abbreviations, and on the first occasion I took the DS notes literally. They read – 'Live rats [rations] will be supplied'! They undertake the usual circuit of varied command tasks, abseil down ropes dangling in the air from a high railway viaduct, and paddle assault boats across a lake by night. Nor are they off the hook when they get back to the Academy as they are bombed out of their trucks a mile away and have to double in and manhandle a burden over the obstacle course. After all this the physical side of the SMC course does not tax them much.

Each cadet writes reports on the performances of all the members in his group, including a self-appraisal. Having been brought up in the strong tradition of loyalty to one's friends I was dubious about this at first, but soon became a strong supporter of the system. It assists them in their functional tasks if they get to know the strengths and weaknesses of their team, as they can then employ them in the roles for which they are best suited. As officers they will have to assess men throughout their careers, so the sooner they are taught to analyse fairly, the better. In general the cadets give honest appraisals, and with six or seven cross-references it is easy to pick out poor judgements. Moreover the system can work to their advantage, as several cadets were given a chance on the SMC when the reports by their peers showed that they took a grip at a stage which could not be observed by the DS.

On the early courses there was a final exercise in Snowdonia, but the cadets consistently said that it just repeated what they had already achieved. We overcame this constructively by sending them to Joint Service Mountain Training Centres to give them a chance to gain a Unit Expedition Leadership certificate. This is the first step towards enabling them to conduct Adventure Training activities with their men on their own.

Rowallan has provided just under a fifth of the intake into SMC courses (until recently the graduates had their own course). Twenty-five per cent pass out in the Above Average category, and three Rowallan men have won the Sword of Honour. It is safe to say that the preliminary training has proved its effectiveness.

A pleasant tradition is that at the end of the course the cadets take all the DS, including myself and the Company clerk, out for a meal. This is preceded by a revue in which the DS (the audience) are satirised. It is a measure of the development of the young men that this is done aptly and amusingly, without overstepping the mark. Equally their bearing in the pub shows that good foundations have been laid to prepare them to become officers. I have had the satisfaction of working with former Rowallan cadets when they have come back as DS Captains, and three of the NCO instructors have been commissioned.

John Adair, a former lecturer at the Academy, introduced the concept of action-centred leadership aimed at achieving a task, building a team and developing individuals. It emphasises the importance of communication, both down and up. A vital but difficult aspect of leadership is delegation of responsibility, so that everyone gets involved. The whole team must be encouraged to take advantage of success, and to learn from mistakes. These principles are useful not only in the Forces, but at all levels of management in industry and other organisations.

A wide variety of extra-mural activities at the Academy are run voluntarily by officers and lecturers. When I arrived, Captain Tony Streather (later the leader of the successful Army expedition which enabled two SAS NCOs to reach the summit of Everest) asked me if I would help him with the Mountaineering and Exploration Club. He was posted a year later, so I found myself in charge of climbing, caving, canoeing and expeditions. The cliffs at Swanage and the rock faces in the Avon gorge were the two areas for climbing within weekend range. The latter could be combined with caving, as the Academy had bought Fountain Cottage in the village of Priddy on the Mendips as a very useful base for the two activities. On long weekends we went down to my old stamping grounds around Land's End – the Cliff Assault course came in useful for peaceful purposes. As the number of expeditions increased it required more and more paper work to get clearances, so I recruited a Captain in each college to give a hand. John Blashford-Snell launched most of the cadet-led expeditions from Old College, and took major Academy parties to Libya and Ethiopia, so it was no surprise to me when he became nationally known for 'Operation Drake' and 'Operation Raleigh'.

From Academy grants I bought some folding Klepper canoes which cadets could take abroad, and got hold of lighter canoes to enable them to enter the Devizes/Westminster race. Canoeing was a specialist sport, with strict safety regulations, and as I was no expert I arranged for a qualified PT instructor to take it over. 'Adventure Training' became the 'buzz' word for promoting leadership, and I readily accepted the suggestion that the Lieutenant Colonel in charge of training should take over the expedition work.

More recently I have helped with major Academy climbing expeditions. In the Canadian Rockies we climbed Mt Lefroy (11,292 ft), just west of Lake Louise. Farther north we reached a position which opened up access to the summit of Mt Robson (12,972 ft), but bad weather and lack of time prevented us from getting to the top.

In 1983 twenty-five of us, including six young men from Sir John Hunt's Endeavour Training organisation, trekked up and down across the grain of the country from Barahbise to Everest Base Camp. Sometimes we had sing-songs round a campfire in the evenings. They enjoyed my Dalmatian and Eighth Army songs, but the dirty verses of 'Little Angeline' interested them most!

After all the heavy load-carrying in northern latitudes it was marvellous to have porters to relieve us of that burden. Higher up above Khumjung sure-footed shaggy yaks carried most of the baggage.

After negotiating the crevasses on the Khumbu glacier we stood far below the massive snow cornices on the Lho La Pass and gazed across at the gigantic frozen cascade of the Everest Icefall. Several of the cadets have since taken part in major Himalayan climbs.

The peak we climbed, Kalar Pattar (18,720 ft), is dwarfed into insignificance by the soaring giants surrounding it, but nevertheless it needed long pauses for breath to reach the top.

In 1987 I accompanied an Academy party which paid an official visit to the Académie Royale Militaire at Meknes in Morocco. Since 1961 they have had a three-year course during which the cadets gain a diploma, mainly in science, maths and languages. French military traditions have been maintained, and the Académie is run by officers and the senior cadets, with very few NCOs or civilians. The officers had had active war experience against Polisario guerrillas in the disputed former Spanish Sahara Territory in the south. An emancipated and attractive young commissioned medical officer was fully accepted in the Mess, but there were no other women.

Everywhere we went we were met by a Guard of Honour. At the Armour Training School I was embarrassed that a whole Regiment had been turned out with their tanks to be inspected by a Captain and nine young cadets. From my time in the ranks I bet that there was some muttering back in the barrack rooms after they had been dismissed, as inevitably they would have been on parade in the hot sun an hour in advance. The Moroccans were proud of their electronically controlled weapons systems, and of their ability to maintain their equipment. The same was true at the Groupe Artillerie Royale depot at Fez, where they had laser and radar range-finding systems. The cadets enjoyed the air defence 'drome' where they manned American fast-firing 20mm cannon guns to fire at aircraft images which are swept across the sky. Hits were electronically recorded.

Throughout the visit our hosts were most hospitable and we dined well, but it was back to self-cooking and camping when we set off again in our Land Rovers and trailers for the High Atlas. Mules came into the picture one more time, as I had made arrangements with Askarrai Lachen, a mountain guide, for them to be available to carry our packs up the Mizane valley to the Nelter climbers' hut. From there we climbed Mt Toubkal, at 13,664 ft the highest peak in North Africa. I made the most of the sweeping views over the Atlas chains and down to the desert in the distance, as at the age of sixty-two I was unlikely to venture as high again.

The motto of the Royal Marines is 'Per Mare Per Terram', and in addition to leading twelve Brathay field-work expeditions and taking part in Academy climbing ventures I crewed on 32-ft and 47-ft yachts in the Strait of Juan de Fuca, among the Leeward Islands in the Caribbean, off Mallorca and Sardinia, and around northern Scotland from Troon to Rosyth.

Events in Northern Ireland, the Falkland Islands, Kuwait and Bosnia have shown that the present generation (women, too, have been successfully integrated into the Officer Training Course at the Academy) can handle threats to Britain's or the world's safety equally as well as we did. We invited a young subaltern in the Parachute Regiment to give a talk to Rowallan cadets on his experiences in the Falklands. He had successfully completed the Rowallan course only three years previously, so he knew exactly how to make the training relevant. Conscious of the physical pressures on Rowallan, he brought along his equipment, loaded with full battle complement of ammunition and other necessities. The cadets were astonished at the weight when they picked it up – and so was I! It reinforced my advice that weapons should not be blazed off unnecessarily.

The Sovereign's Parade is an impressive display of military precision, and it is a moving ceremony too as the Senior Intake turns inward and slow-marches up the steps of Old College to pass through the massive black doors to the haunting strains of 'Auld Lang Syne'. They are followed by the Adjutant on his white charger, who clatters up the steps and through the door with plenty of room to spare. On the last parade that I attended the Major General who was Commandant of the Academy had been a Junior Under Officer in the Company to which I had been attached when I first arrived. The wheel had turned full circle.

My fifty years of close association with the Armed Forces have been rewarding. Wartime training taught me how to look after myself properly, and enabled me to deal with difficult situations. At Sandhurst I passed on what I had learned about man-management in the hope that it would help to mould the cadets into officers who will look after the interests of their men. The climbing, caving and sailing activities brought out the need for mutual support, and showed how comradeship develops informally. On Brathay expeditions the young men discovered that they could survive in difficult terrain with what they could carry on their backs, though they came to realise that it needed careful planning of food dumps. All of them responded well to the discipline of achieving accurate field-work in metereology, botany, ornithology, geology, archaeology and surveying. They developed a professional determination to complete the tasks despite having to endure spells of freezing temperatures, blanketing snow, soaking rain and piercing winds. Leadership qualities can be improved through training, but it pays to have a sense of humour.

Clothing and Equipment, October 1944

Key to abbreviations

BD   battledress. amn – ammunition.

PIAT   Projector Infantry Anti-tank. This was a lighter close-range weapon which replaced the annoyingly heavy, awkward and useless Boyes Anti-tank Rifle. It fired a rounded bomb with a thin nose and a tail-fin from a semi-circular cupped holder, with a shoulder pad to the rear and a stand in the middle.

LMG   Light Machine Gun (Bren). Fired .303 bullets from slightly curved magazines.

2-in M   Mortar with 2-in barrel. Consisted of tube, and base-plate with firing pin.

WB   Water bottle.

KD   Khaki Drill. Tropical shirts and shorts.

CMF   Central Mediterranean Forces.

Move of 43 (RM) CDO from VIS   TOP SECRET

There is a possibility that the Cdo will move from VIS within a day or two. Fighting personnel may have to go tactically dressed and equipped, for an immediate transfer to another theatre of operations. Weather in this new theatre is known to be inclement.

Dress and Packing of Equipment

a)   2nd best BD, face veils worn round necks scarf position
          Berets
          Boots and gaiters
          Mae Wests
          Weapons and operational amn (normal scale on man)
          2-in Mortar and amn, PIATS and amn in Tp dumps to go with Tp
          LMG mags in boxes with 2-in M and PIATS

b)   **Marching Order** plus entrenching tools, WB on right side
Gas cape rolled above large pack, leather jerkin rolled up inside
In large pack
    Ground sheet
    1 blanket
    Change of underwear
    Spare socks
    Laces
    1 pr denims
In small pack
    Mess tin, knife, fork and spoon
    Washing and shaving gear
    Cleaning gear
    Pullover
    Cap comforter

c)   **ST kitbag** (to go into Rear HQ store, and NOT be readily available)
Steel Helmet
Best BD
Slippers
Personal effects

d)   **AP kitbag** (to be available for bringing over to Tps, as soon as possible if Cdo goes on an Operation, or taken with the Cdo)
Greatcoat
Felt soled boots
Remaining underclothes and socks
Spare pair boots
Spare denims

e)   **All Tps** to have blankets in 3 man rolls. Blankets and rolls to be marked. (9 blankets)

f)   **All KD**, except puttees, to be returned to QM by Tps on call from QM. Any deficiencies in winter clothing will be made up if possible prior to leaving VIS.

CMF 9 Oct 44

                            George FROST
                            Capt & Adjt.

162nd (Turkoman) Infantry Division

This unit was originally formed by grouping a number of Pomeranian and Mecklenburger replacement-training units under the newly formed divisional headquarters in January 1940. It took part in the first campaigns in Russia and was continuously engaged from June 1941 until the first winter offensive was checked in early 1942. The 162nd suffered serious losses before Moscow in December 1941 and later served on the southern sector of the Eastern Front until the autumn of 1942. Its commander at this time was Major General Professor Doctor Oscar Ritter von Niedermayer, a well-known specialist in foreign affairs. Perhaps for this reason the 162nd was selected to train Ost (Eastern) battalions, which were established by the order of the High Command in late 1941. These troops – including people from Georgia, Armenia, Azerbaijan, Kazak, Turkestan, Iran, Afghanistan and others – all volunteered to fight in German service against Communism. After they left the 162nd these battalions (collectively called 'Turks') were sent to other active divisions. The 162nd initially set up training operations in Poland but in early 1943 was transferred to Slovenia, where it simultaneously conducted training and anti-Partisan operations along the Ljubljana–Trieste railroad. Early in 1944 the division was transferred to Army Detachment von Zangen in northern Italy and was given the mission of guarding the Ligurian coast. By this time most of its personnel were non-Germans, and its veterans of the Russian Front had been transferred to other units. In June 1944 it was briefly committed to action on the Italian Front but was withdrawn due to its poor performance. It was again sent into action in October and was withdrawn again for the same reason. The division spent the rest of the war fighting partisans in the mountains north-east of La Spezia and later in the Tavo Valley, Italy. The 162nd surrendered to the Western Allies in 1945. Many of its personnel were turned over to the Russians after the war and disappeared.

Turkoman Flag taken at Comacchio

The flag is 32 in × 14 in, with a V cut in on the right, giving it two pennant tips. There is a pale yellow upper band, with two badges dyed into the material, and the lower half of the flag is red. In the top left badge there is an arm holding a scimitar in a red square which has a blue and yellow puffed sleeve above the elbow, leaving the forearm bare. The slightly curved broadening blade points to the rear, poised for a slash. Four red arrows outlined in black burst outwards from the corners of the square. To the right an eagle is emblazoned on a red shield. Its wings are spread; its tail curves down between outstretched talons; its yellow beak points to the left with tongue curled upward; and there is a yellow crown on its head.

The unit shoulder-badge, which I also acquired, is a shield on a grey background with TURKISTAN embroidered at the top. The upper half of the shield is red, the lower half blue, and in the centre is a short white bow with a long arrow crossing right. There are three curves in the thick middle part of the shaft of the bow, and the extremities curve slightly outward where the perpendicular string is attached. Maybe this is based on the bows used by Jenghis Khan's men during his Mongol conquests.

APPENDIX 3

The Brathay Exploration Group

Since 1947 the Brathay Exploration Group has been providing opportunities for young people to explore the world, and in so doing to develop their own potential. Brathay expeditions have clear objectives involving worthwhile tasks of discovery and exploration set in wild and remote regions of the British Isles and around the world.

The Group has gained wide recognition for its ability to tackle scientific fieldwork and environmental and social investigations, and to bring back data of value to research. Such tasks have taken members from the snow and ice of the Arctic to tropical rainforests, from deserts to rocky coastlines, and to the margins of human settlements in high mountains and remote islands.

Young people are a country's most precious asset, but their abilities and confidence need discovering, strengthening and testing. The Brathay Exploration Group provides a wide range of demanding experiences that can do this, while also developing tolerance, teamwork and understanding. The practical experience of taking part in ventures to remote and wild country poses a powerful educational challenge.

The Group was the first to bring together school sixth-formers and industrial trainees in its expedition teams – to mutual benefit. It pioneered combining youngsters from the United Kingdom with their counterparts in host countries, particularly in Uganda and Kenya in the early 1960s, and Eastern Europe and China more recently, where the projects undertaken were relevant to those countries' interests. Women leaders and girls have been fully integrated into expeditions since the 1970s, and some handicapped and disadvantaged young people have been given support to enable them to play an active part. The Group was a joint founder, with the British Schools Exploring Society, of the Young Explorers' Trust, set up in 1972, which has done so much to promote wider opportunities for youthful ventures.

The Exploration Group owes its origins to the Brathay Hall Trust founded by Francis Scott, Chairman of the Provincial Insurance Company, and a man of great vision. He had purchased in 1939 the 300-acre Brathay estate on the northern shore of Windermere in the Lake District, to preserve it in the public interest. The educational trust which was to play such an important part in pioneering the concept of 'development training' was established in 1946. The

Outward Bound Trust was founded in the same year and both sought to discover peacetime challenges, replacing but learning from wartime experiences.

From the first experimental courses at Brathay Hall there emerged a project – the Tarn Surveys – to sound the uncharted mountain lakes of the Lake District. This information was urgently needed by those undertaking research into the effect of glaciers on mountain landscapes, notably Vaughan Lewis of the Cambridge Geography Department, who did so much to promote and support the project. The task proved ideal, posing challenges in constructing light craft to be carried into the hills, learning the basics of planetable survey, and from a mountain camp undertaking accurate recording of water depths. The revelation in 1948 of the unexpected depth of Blea Water was a significant geographical discovery. This small mountain tarn, situated at a height of 1584 feet near Haweswater, had a maximum depth of 207 feet – almost as deep as the 11-mile-long Windermere. This discovery aroused much interest, not least in demonstrating a valuable potential role for young explorers.

By 1951 charts had been made of more than thirty mountain tarns. Many voluntary leaders, some like Bill Jenkins with highly relevant Service experience, had become involved in the project, attracted by the possibilities of an expanding programme of adventurous exploration and discovery. Teachers were well represented, helping to build up wide contacts in schools. So it came about that from the outset expedition teams were drawn both from school sixth forms and from young trainees in industry, following a course at Brathay Hall. The broad social mix and the blend of the academic and practical approaches proved a great success.

In 1951 a new programme of 26-day courses for young industrial trainees at Brathay Hall offered a distinctive approach to all-round personal development through adventurous hillcraft and sailing activities blending with opportunities for creative art and drama. Meanwhile the Trustees agreed to build for the now independent Brathay Exploration Group separate headquarters with accommodation and equipment storage facilities in the Brathay estate. The Group's programme of expeditions was organised by a team of Honorary Officers, advised and supported by a Council, which included well-known people from universities, schools and industry. With the help of the Council the whole spectrum of project ideas was expanded, doors to new opportunities were opened, and essential contacts both at home and abroad were provided.

At the invitation of the Cambridge Glaciological Research Programme, Brathay parties became involved in Norway in exciting tasks investigating glacier structure and movement. These were essentially practical projects, set in challenging high mountains and contributing significantly to a major research initiative. This work culminated in a detailed study undertaken by the Group of Tunsbergdalsbre, Norway's longest glacier, and led to similar studies in Iceland and Greenland.

By 1960 a clear pattern of expeditions had evolved. This consisted of six one-week basic expedition training ventures in the Lake District; four parties visiting Britain's remotest inhabited island, Foula, for long-term ornithological studies and support of the island community; and at least three major overseas expeditions. There was a firm tradition (a) that expedition teams should be small (maximum size twenty), with not more than two members from any one school or firm, and (b) that once appointed each main Leader accepted full responsibility for planning the venture and leading it in the field. Overseas expeditions were of three to four weeks' duration.

The development of new projects in Africa in the 1960s added an important dimension to the expedition programme. In Tunisia archaeological investigations on the edge of the Sahara yielded significant discoveries over eight seasons. In Kenya and Uganda, in close cooperation with indigenous research institutes, a fascinating programme of exploration projects was developed, in which equal numbers of UK members and young Africans took part. This led to the setting up of a Kenya Exploring Society, of which Richard Leakey was chairman.

The establishment in 1967 of a Field Study Centre in a second large house on the Brathay estate provided a much needed focus and planning base for the Group, with library facilities, storage of maps and records, and maintenance of survey and scientific equipment. For twenty years the Centre's professional staff ran one-week courses for A-level students in biology, geography and geology, interspersed with university field courses organised by their own staff. During this period and especially in its second decade when the two complementary activities combined to become the Centre for Exploration and Field Studies, the Group's expedition programme reached a peak of achievement. Some 300 members took part in up to twenty expeditions annually. New venues for exploration projects included wilderness areas in the Canadian Rockies, rain forests in Central and South America, game reserves in Zimbabwe, glacier treks in Spitzbergen, and ecological studies in Jamaica and Cyprus. Of particular importance was a major project, fully sponsored by BP, to devise methods for monitoring the ecology of remote rocky coasts in Arctic Norway, where the threat of oil pollution exists.

Major policy changes within the Brathay Hall Trust, involving a move into the training of managers as the first priority, had an adverse effect on the Group. The decline in work with young people, and most regrettably, the decision to close the Field Study Centre, left the Exploration Group isolated and without the strong support it had enjoyed for so long from the parent Trust.

In 1989 the Exploration Group became independent of the Brathay Hall Trust, and a new Charitable Trust has been set up. Vigorous action by voluntary leaders and an enthusiastic and expanding membership are leading to a comeback. In 1995 Brathay expeditions ventured to the mountains of Sichuan in western China, the Amazonia tropical forest, Lapland, Jotunheim National Park, the French Alps and a first expedition to Bulgaria. A Mountain First Aid Course was run from the Brathay base in the Lake District, and Leader Training Courses were held in the Cairngorms.

In summary, the objectives of the Brathay Exploration Group have been to widen horizons; enhance personal and social development; develop cross-cultural understanding; stimulate environmental awareness; teach practical skills; and contribute useful data towards research.

Further information may be obtained from the Administrator, Brathay Exploration Group, Brathay Hall, Ambleside, Cumbria LA22 0HP.

Bibliography

'A history of the period of Active Service of 43 Royal Marine Commando in the Central Mediterranean Forces until the end of the war in Italy.' Copied type-written script issued to members of the Unit in 1945.

'History of the Commandos in the Mediterranean September 1943 to May 1945.' (Bound copies of Operation Orders with an accompanying script. Limited distribution.)

Churchill, Winston S. *The Second World War*. 6 vols. Cassell, 1949.

Deakin, F.W.D. *The Embattled Mountain*. OUP, 1971.

Jackson, General Sir William. *The Mediterranean and Middle East*. HMSO, 1988. Volume VI, Part III of the *Official Histories of the Second World War*.

Maclean, Fitzroy. *Eastern Approaches*. Jonathan Cape, 1949.

Maclean, Fitzroy. *Disputed Barricade*. Jonathan Cape, 1957.

McConville, Michael. *A Small War in the Balkans*. Macmillan, 1986.

McConville, Michael. *Nothing Much to Lose*. Privately printed, 1992. (The wartime history of 2nd Battalion Royal Marines and 43 Commando Royal Marines.)

Messenger, Charles. *The Commandos 1940–1946*. William Kimber, 1985.

Saunders, Hilary St George. *The Green Beret*. Michael Joseph, 1949.

Index